The Son of Man in Mark's Gospel

Australian College of Theology Monograph Series

SERIES EDITOR GRAEME R. CHATFIELD

The ACT Monograph Series, generously supported by the Board of Directors of the Australian College of Theology, provides a forum for publishing quality research theses and studies by its graduates and affiliated college staff in the broad fields of Biblical Studies, Christian Thought and History, and Practical Theology with Wipf and Stock Publishers of Eugene, Oregon. The ACT selects the best of its doctoral and research masters theses as well as monographs that offer the academic community, scholars, church leaders and the wider community uniquely Australian and New Zealand perspectives on significant research topics and topics of current debate. The ACT also provides opportunity for contributors beyond its graduates and affiliated college staff to publish monographs which support the mission and values of the ACT.

Rev Dr Graeme Chatfield
Series Editor and Associate Dean

The Son of Man in Mark's Gospel

Exploring its Possible Connections with
the Book of Ezekiel

DAVID FORREST MITCHELL

WIPF & STOCK · Eugene, Oregon

THE SON OF MAN IN MARK'S GOSPEL
Exploring its Possible Connections with the Book of Ezekiel

Australian College of Theology Monograph Series

Copyright © 2019 David Forrest Mitchell. All rights reserved. Except for brief quotations in critical publications or reviews, no part of this book may be reproduced in any manner without prior written permission from the publisher. Write: Permissions, Wipf and Stock Publishers, 199 W. 8th Ave., Suite 3, Eugene, OR 97401.

Wipf & Stock
An Imprint of Wipf and Stock Publishers
199 W. 8th Ave., Suite 3
Eugene, OR 97401

www.wipfandstock.com

PAPERBACK ISBN: 978-1-7252-5657-6
HARDCOVER ISBN: 978-1-7252-5658-3
EBOOK ISBN: 978-1-7252-5659-0

Quotations of the original languages have been taken from:

Biblia Hebraica Stuttgartensia: SESB Version, electronic ed. Stuttgart: German Bible Society, 2003.

The Greek New Testament, 5th Rev. ed. Stuttgart: Deutsche Bibelgesellschaft, 2014.

Septuaginta: With Morphology, electronic ed. Stuttgart: Deutsche Bibelgesellschaft, 1979.

Manufactured in the U.S.A.   NOVEMBER 21, 2019

All glory and honor, meagre as it might be, must go to the God who not only made me, but has also loved and redeemed me through his Son Jesus Christ, by the power of his Holy Spirit. Under God, I want to dedicate this book to my wife Traci. Though she has not read it, and probably never will, it would never have come together without her support.

Contents

Preface | ix
Acknowledgements | xi
Abbreviations | xii

1 Current State of Son of Man Scholarship and the Thesis of This Book | 1
    The Problem and Why There are So Many "Solutions" | 1
    Four Views in Current Scholarship | 4
    Can There Be an Overlapping Solution? | 9
    The Contribution of This Book to the Scholarship | 10

2 Methodological Questions | 12
    An Alternative Order of Argument | 12
    Justification for the Exegetical Approach Taken | 13

3 The Son of Man in Mark | 17
    Mark 2:1–12 | 17
    Mark 2:23–28 | 20
    Mark 8:27—9:1 | 25
    Mark 9:9–13 | 30
    Mark 9:30–32 | 35
    Mark 10:32–45 | 38
    Mark 13:24–37 | 43
    Mark 14:17–25 | 47
    Mark 14:32–52 | 50
    Mark 14:53–65 | 53

4   Synthesis of the Markan Son of Man | 57

5   Why Ezekiel Deserves Some Further Interaction | 62
    Reopening the Door | 62
    Danielic Background and Its Limitations | 63
    Awareness of Ezekiel and Hebrew Language | 66
    Singular and Definite Son of Man | 69
    Conclusion | 70

6   Ezekiel's בֶּן־אָדָם | 72
    Introduction | 72
    What Does בֶּן־אָדָם Convey? | 72
    The Effect of Calling Ezekiel בֶּן־אָדָם | 74
    Conclusion | 79

7   Comparing the Ezekielic בֶּן־אָדָם to the Markan ὁ υἱὸς τοῦ ἀνθρώπου | 81
    Points of Similarity | 81
    Points of Dissimilarity | 83
    Conclusion | 84

8   Evaluation of the Relationship between the Two Sons of Man | 86

9   Final Conclusion | 91

    Bibliography | 95

Preface

Jesus's chosen self-designation must be considered important for anyone who wishes to know the authentic Jesus, let alone rely on him for salvation. It is my hope and prayer that this book might help those who wish to engage deeply (though, it must be said, in a rather technical, i.e. nerdy way), not simply with the topic and its associated themes, but with Jesus himself.

This work is a very slightly edited version of the thesis I submitted as part of a Master of Theology through the Australian College of Theology affiliated Trinity Theological College in Perth, Western Australia. I began that work on three basic premises: I wanted to hone my skills in thorough biblical exegesis both in Greek and Hebrew; I wanted to work in the Gospels (since I had not done so in the final year of my Bachelor of Theology degree); and, in particular, I wanted to explore that intriguing self-designation of Jesus, ὁ υἱὸς τοῦ ἀνθρώπου, Son of Man. Eventually the idea for a thesis was narrowed to a technical examination of the topic described in the title: explore the Son of Man in Mark's Gospel and examine whether there might be a case for some background in Ezekiel.

Having completed the body of work almost a year ago and receiving some excellent feedback from supervisors, I look back now thinking that there is more that could have been done to strengthen aspects of the argument, or better engage those with whom I would differ. Without apologizing for the content herein—I stand by it—the main areas I would have extended would be in a deeper discussion of the interrelation of Daniel and Ezekiel and what it might mean for Jesus's undeniable association with the Danielic vision, a more thorough engagement with Mark's kingdom of God motif, and a biblical-theological development of a "son of man" concept which finds its climax and fulfillment in Jesus. Without wishing to substantially alter the argument, nor extend the length of the book dramatically, such matters will have to wait for another time.

Acknowledgements

ASIDE FROM MY SUPERVISOR, Dr. Allan Chapple, and co-supervisor, Dr. David Seccombe, and the rest of the Trinity Theological College staff, I would also like to acknowledge the help provided in proofreading and suggestions by my mum, Rosemary Mitchell, and by my friends Beth Webb and Daniel Faricy. The Anglican Diocese of North Western Australia and my parish of Dongara-Mingenew were both encouraging of my study and made time available for this work.

Abbreviations

AB	Anchor Bible
ABRL	Anchor Bible Reference Library
AT	*Annales Theologici*
BBR	*Bulletin for Biblical Research*
BDAG	Danker, Frederick W., Walter Bauer, William F. Arndt, and F. Wilbur Gingrich. *Greek-English Lexicon of the New Testament and Other Early Christian Literature*. 3rd ed. Chicago: University of Chicago Press, 2000 (Danker-Bauer-Arndt-Gingrich)
BECNT	Baker Exegetical Commentary on the New Testament
BETL	Bibliotheca Ephemeridum Theologicarum Lovaniensium
BibSem	The Biblical Seminar
BN	*Biblische Notizen*
BNTC	Black's New Testament Commentary
CBQ	*Catholic Biblical Quarterly*
HUCA	*Hebrew Union College Annual*
JBL	*Journal of Biblical Literature*
JJS	*Journal of Jewish Studies*
JSNTSup	Journal for the Study of the New Testament, Supplement Series
LNTS	The Library of New Testament Studies
NAC	New American Commentary

NICNT	New International Commentary on the New Testament
NICOT	New International Commentary on the Old Testament
NIGTC	New International Greek Testament Commentary
NIV2011	The New International Version (Grand Rapids, MI: Zondervan, 2011)
NIVAC	NIV Application Commentary
NSBT	New Studies in Biblical Theology
PNTC	Pillar New Testament Commentary
SHBC	Smyth & Helwys Bible Commentary
SNTSMS	Society for New Testament Studies Monograph Series
SNTW	Studies of the New Testament and Its World
TDNT	*Theological Dictionary of the New Testament*. Edited by Gerhard Kittel and Gerhard Friedrich. Translated by Geoffrey W. Bromiley. 10 vols. Grand Rapids: Eerdmans, 1964–1976
TDOT	*Theological Dictionary of the Old Testament*. Edited by G. Johannes Botterweck and Helmer Ringgren. Translated by John T. Willis et al. 8 vols. Grand Rapids: Eerdmans, 1974–2006
WBC	Word Biblical Commentary
ZECNT	Zondervan Exegetical Commentary of the New Testament
ZNW	*Zeitschrift für die neutestamentliche Wissenschaft und die Kunde der älteren Kirche*

I

Current State of Son of Man Scholarship and the Thesis of This Book

WHILE IT IS USEFUL to begin by setting the scene for Son of Man scholarship, the data related to Jesus's use of ὁ υἱὸς τοῦ ἀνθρώπου is both so large and variegated that this chapter could hardly do justice to it. There are however, two recent major monographs that cover such matters in detail—Delbert Burkett's *The Son of Man Debate: A History and Evaluation* and Mogens Müller's *The Expression "Son of Man" and Development of Christology*.[1] Burkett's is a more thematic approach, cataloguing the various views under headings, though in general it does progress from the church fathers through to the current situation. Müller aims at a more diachronic approach, writing "a history of interpretation to show the interaction between the various periods' christology and its impact on their interpretation of the expression Son of man."[2] What can be achieved, by way of introduction, is to describe the nature of the "Son of Man problem," why so many mutually exclusive, yet defendable, solutions arise, and the four broad positions currently held in scholarship. Following this overview, the proposed argument of this book will be put forward.

The Problem and Why There are So Many "Solutions"

Why did Jesus call himself the Son of Man and what did he mean by it? This is the most foundational question to answer, but the difficulty in answering this question—the reason why there is a so-called "Son of Man

1. Burkett, *Son of Man Debate*; Müller, *Expression Son of Man*.
2. Müller, *Expression Son of Man*, vii.

problem"—can have the main points of debate summarized under four headings of concern: historical, form, inherent meaning, and background. The historical concern can be captured by this puzzling question: Why, when the Jesus of the Gospels regularly uses the phrase for himself, is Son of Man so rarely used of Jesus in the earliest proclamations about him? Outside of the Gospels it is hardly used in the New Testament, yet Lord, Christ, and Son of God, for example, are used throughout. Additionally, there are many scholars who question which of the Son of Man sayings from the Gospels should be considered completely authentic to the historical Jesus and which might be reconstructions, or even inventions, from the compilers of the Gospels. Most scholars agree that the phrase has its origins on the lips of Jesus, but its transmission into the New Testament, and the reasons for that transmission, are a major source of division in scholarship.

The second concern questions how the form of ὁ υἱὸς τοῦ ἀνθρώπου should be understood. It is certainly unique, since this singular, double-article form of a "son of man" phrase has no precedent in any extant Greek work,[3] and thus there is some need to account for the form of the phrase itself. Given the use of the articles, scholars have tended to understand it as a title, similar in form to, though different in meaning from, Son of God. Many have considered its form odd enough to be non-Greek, or at least not "natural Greek," and this consideration then drove scholars to look for a Semitic background, most commonly an Aramaic one. While this brought new options for the sense of it as a title, it led others to conclude that it was more simply an idiom. The nature of a presumed contemporaneous idiom has been debated (see below), but the prolific and influential Maurice Casey went further and not only translated the phrase back into Aramaic but entire sayings as well, thus changing the platform of the debate entirely because of his concerns about form. The debate around form remains wide open and, since function is contingent on form, the meaning of ὁ υἱὸς τοῦ ἀνθρώπου cannot be regarded as settled.

This leads to the third point for debate: the inherent meaning of ὁ υἱὸς τοῦ ἀνθρώπου. Those who consider it to be idiomatic often describe its meaning as a circumlocution for the first-person pronoun, or a general reference to a "human," or a reference to people in general and Jesus (and his disciples) in particular. Those who have read the phrase more literally would argue that it would be better translated as "son of a human" or "Son of Adam." Others think the phrase conveys a sense of humanity, humility, mortality and lowliness. Still others consider it a more lofty, if not immediately

---

3. This is a point for discussion in chs. 5 and 6; also cf. Hurtado, "Summary and Concluding Observations," 159–77.

obvious, title, claiming power and authority. As Driver wrote over a century ago, "it ought to be clearly understood that it is not anywhere *explained* in the NT, so that whatever view of it be adopted must be a matter of conjecture and inference."[4] Müller recently concurred, "There is no obvious point of departure for understanding."[5]

The fourth problem relates to the background. Where did the phrase and its meaning come from? Any idiomatic interpretation, mentioned above, must assume a close Semitic background. But if the phrase is not an idiom, or something more than generally idiomatic, then it is possible, even likely, that the Gospels' Son of Man is building on some preexisting concept. Mark 13:26 and 14:62 (with parallels) offer clear allusions to Daniel 7:13, though scholars debate the authenticity of these texts in relation to the historical Jesus. Even where the background is agreed, the nature of this background is often debated. Does a Danielic Son of Man, for example, provide a complete background for the Son of Man concept in the Gospels, or is it greatly expanded upon? And how well established in the contemporary thought environment (when Jesus delivered the sayings or when the Gospels were written) was any given background? While 1 Enoch 37–71 and 4 Ezra 13 offer a "son of man" in an apocalyptic judgment setting, their dating and relevance as background for the Gospels' Son of Man is questionable.[6] Again, the lack of agreement about sources and background will necessarily cause contention regarding both the form and the function of the phrase.

Given scholars have approached the question through a particular field of research within one or more of these points of history, form, inherent meaning and background, have found multiple ways to answer the questions each point raises, and have used results in one area to draw conclusions in another, it is not surprising that there seem to be as many answers to the Son of Man problem as there are scholars to answer it. The rediscovery of biblical languages by Western scholars five centuries ago, the discovery and subsequent translation of the Similitudes of 1 Enoch and the discovery of the Qumran texts five decades ago mark the biggest turning points in scholarship. Though a number of false paths have long been abandoned, scholarship remains well divided on all these issues. "Study of the mysterious synoptic title, 'the Son of man,' has become a specialized field of its own wherein scholarly discord reigns supreme . . . the ever-mushrooming

---

4. Driver, "Son of Man," 584, emphasis original; so also Müller, *Expression Son of Man*, 1–2.

5. Müller, *Expression Son of Man*, 2.

6. Burkett, *Son of Man Debate*, 97–120. The need for a reexamination of a possible background in Ezekiel will be discussed in ch. 5.

literature on the Son of man offers a host of conflicting and sometimes confusing claims and counter claims."[7]

Four Views in Current Scholarship

Originally a Nontitular Idiom

Virtually all scholars agree that in Semitic contexts, the phrasing "son of man" is at the core a poetic way of speaking about a human, but there are key scholars who think that this is really the only sense the phrase had until the composition of the Gospels and subsequent Greco-Christian interpretation. In this view the historical Jesus was only using a common idiom that may have been a turn of phrase, but nothing more. There are three broad categories for understanding the sense of the idiom: circumlocutional (i.e. Son of Man stands for I), generic (Son of Man stands for humanity), and indefinite (Son of Man stands for a man).

There have been many proponents of variations of this theory stretching back hundreds of years,[8] but none more prolific or influential for current scholarship than the late Maurice Casey. Casey's "solution" depended upon examination of the use of בר אנשא and its variants in Aramaic sources. He concluded that the idiom could have a "general and specific level of meaning."[9] "The intended reference may be to the speaker, or to the speaker and a group of associates, or to another person made obvious by the context."[10] After retrotranslating the Gospels' sayings into Aramaic, Casey determined which could credibly be considered utterances of the real, Aramaic speaking, Jesus. "[W]hen examples of this idiomatic usage emerge from the reconstruction of Aramaic sources from our Gospel sayings, they should be accepted as genuine examples of this idiom."[11] Casey then argued that ὁ υἱὸς τοῦ ἀνθρώπου was a reasonable translation of the authentic sayings, conveying especially the primary sense of self-reference Jesus used.

Whatever the specific meaning of the idiom, an idiomatic view must account for the seemingly titular nature of the saying in the New Testament. Müller describes the process simply, "Although a more or less colourless

---

7. Davies and Allison, *Critical and Exegetical Commentary*, 43.

8. E.g. Bèze, *Novum Testamentum*, at Matt 8:20; Schweizer, "Der Menschensohn"; Dodd, *Founder of Christianity*, 110–13; Vermès, *Jesus the Jew*, 160–91; "Present State"; "Son of Man"; Lindars, *Jesus, Son of Man*.

9. Casey, *Solution*, 314.

10. Casey, *Solution*, 314–15.

11. Casey, *Solution*, 315.

circumlocution in its origin, in the Gospels [Son of Man] gained a certain content through its placement in the construction of the story of the earthly Jesus as the Messiah."[12] From Casey's perspective this was not so much a failure to translate clearly,[13] as much as a beneficial coincidence which allowed the Gospel writers "to satisfy the need of the target culture to express the centrality of Jesus"[14] by expanding the Son of Man sayings to point to a second coming according to Daniel 7:13. Thus, Casey's argument runs, only after the awareness of the original, nontitular understanding of Son of Man was lost in the church was there a problem with interpretation.

Substantial critique of the idiomatic view in general, and Casey in particular, has been offered by both Burkett's monograph and the series of essays in "Who is This Son of Man?,"[15] but here critique will necessarily be succinct. The most significant problem for Casey, and any idiomatic approach, remains the implied dichotomy required between the Greek of the New Testament and its proposed Aramaic background. Even if the Gospel writers thought that they were offering a literal translation which could be used in a titular way, there needs to be some sense in which they failed to convey this meaning since the church in subsequent generations quickly misunderstood ὁ υἱὸς τοῦ ἀνθρώπου as a title. A circumlocution theory also fails to account for why Greek writers would not have used a demonstrative pronoun (e.g. *this* son of man), while the generic and indefinite positions require the exclusion of all but a few sayings, since there is no other way to account for the fact that Jesus is the only one to use the expression and clearly uses it to refer exclusively to himself (though see below).[16] An Aramaic *Vorlage* is by no means certain, and even if it were, its precise form and meaning are not settled.[17] Casey's work is dependent on Aramaic being stable across dialects and through a number of centuries, but Owen questions his evidence for this especially in regard to the force of the Aramaic "emphatic state" in Jesus's presumed use of the phrase בר אנשא.[18] Furthermore, Casey's approach relies on a specific interpretation of Daniel 7, in which "son of man" is symbolic of the saints, as well as a complete dismissal of any messianic association with Son of Man, but neither of these positions is certain.

12. Müller, *Expression Son of Man*, 419.
13. Contra Burkett, *Son of Man Debate*, 90.
14. Casey, *Solution*, 317.
15. Burkett, *Son of Man Debate*, esp. ch. 8; Hurtado and Owen, *Who Is This?*, esp. chs. 1–5, 8.
16. Burkett, *Son of Man Debate*, 87, 92–96.
17. Lukaszewski, "Issues Concerning the Aramaic."
18. Owen, "Problems."

Casey's extensive scholarship and effort in the original languages should be applauded, and his work has helped to show flaws in the "apocalyptic Son of Man" theory (see below). However, Burkett's conclusion captures the chief response for those who differ on the idiomatic interpretations on offer: "The scholars who have investigated the nontitular explanation have performed a service for the scholarly community. It was a possibility that had to be explored and has been well explored. The time has come, however, to take stock and recognize that this line of research has not led to a convincing solution."[19]

Originally Titular Which Jesus Used of Someone Else

Another solution for Son of Man is that Jesus was referring specifically to someone else. Jesus promised that God's kingdom would come in some great apocalyptic way but "talked about someone else, rather than himself, as the coming Son of Man."[20] "Until the late 1960s this reconstruction was one of the most widely accepted solutions of the problem."[21] Bultmann was the most influential in promoting this view,[22] but due to the widely read Bart Ehrman,[23] it remains popular today.[24]

As with the idiomatic interpretation, this view needs to exclude a lot of sayings from Jesus which are unambiguously self-referential as inventions of the church. It faces further issues since it depends on Mark 8:38, which speaks of the coming Son of Man, but this passage is considered by some scholars to be a postresurrection saying brought back into an earlier setting.[25] It also depends on a fairly well established expectation of an apocalyptic Son of Man to which Jesus would have been referring, and "many scholars have come to believe that no such expectation existed in pre-Christian Judaism."[26] Howard Marshall summarizes the primary points of concern:

> The evidence that [Jesus] was really speaking about somebody else rests solely on the alleged distinction found in Luke 12:8f. (*cf.* Mk. 8:38), Mark 14:62 and Matthew 19:28. None of these

19. Burkett, *Son of Man Debate*, 96.
20. Ehrman, *How Jesus Became God*, 119, cf. 121.
21. Burkett, *Son of Man Debate*, 38.
22. Bultmann, *Synoptic Tradition*.
23. Ehrman, *How Jesus Became God* is cited widely online.
24. For a discussion of the (mostly German) proponents of this theory through history see Burkett, *Son of Man Debate*, 37–39 and Müller, *Expression Son of Man*, 287–91.
25. Burkett, *Son of Man Debate*, 38–39.
26. Burkett, *Son of Man Debate*, 39.

texts demands to be interpreted in this way, and it is clear that the early church did not think that they referred to somebody else, nor did it find them sufficiently ambiguous to need reformulation. . . . The defenders of this view have the utmost difficulty in explaining how Jesus visualized the relationship between himself and this shadowy figure.[27]

Originally Titular and Largely Invented by the Church

A third option is that the phrase was originally titular but has been largely invented by the church. This view would fit well with a lot of critical scholarship which interprets Jesus's use of "Son" and "Son of God" in the same way. This depends on there being some regard for Daniel 7 as a background source, but it does not necessarily require an established tradition in Judaism. Instead the New Testament itself can be thought of as establishing a christological interpretation of Daniel 7 and a wider Son of Man ministry. Thus, while the church may have been faithfully capturing its own proclamation of Jesus and even Jesus's own teaching about his authority, death, and resurrection, and coming judgment, this view places the interpretation of Son of Man squarely on the church. Burkett describes a possible method of progression: "as early Jewish Christians spoke about Jesus as the Son of Man, this title came to be retrojected onto the lips of Jesus . . . preserved and even augmented in the further development of the tradition."[28]

This view does just allow for possible historical authenticity of the phrase on the lips of Jesus. "Even if it were certain, however, that all of the Son of Man sayings originated in the early church, we could not be certain about the title 'Son of Man' itself,"[29] but even Burkett recognizes that the "primary objection to this conclusion has been the fact that almost all Son of Man sayings occur on the lips of Jesus."[30] While retrojection is not quite the same as a failure to properly communicate (as the idiomatic view sees the New Testament), nor a corruption of Jesus's meaning (as the third-person view sees it), this view still holds that most—if not all—the sayings are non-historical in their Gospel settings.

One of the problems that this theory must account for is why the phrase is not used outside of the Gospels. Burkett's response is that the "absence of the title 'Son of Man' . . . can be best explained if the title had currency

27. Marshall, *New Testament Christology*, 73.
28. Burkett, *Son of Man Debate*, 56.
29. Burkett, *Son of Man Debate*, 124.
30. Burkett, *Son of Man Debate*, 56.

primarily in Palestinian Christianity. . . . If the title 'Son of Man' arose in a Palestinian context, it should appear precisely where it does."[31] Perhaps this is so, but it does not seem to fit with the recent trend in scholarship that recognizes Paul's Jewish concerns, and his concerns for a consistent presentation of the gospel. It also fails to account for why New Testament letters written to predominantly gentile churches were so prevalent in their use of "Son of God," but omit Son of Man. The former definitively has a Jewish background and can only properly be understood in relation to that background. Both must have had "currency" among Palestinian Christianity, but why did only one make it beyond Palestine? Additionally, while this theory provides time for the motif to be developed, which may explain why Son of Man does not appear in the Epistles, it does not seem to account for the context of Mark's composition, which has mostly been considered Greco-Roman,[32] thus begging the question why he would so readily include something which belonged to a different context and was not authentic to Jesus in the first place.

Originally Titular, Self-Referring, and Well Preserved by the Gospels

The final position tends to be the more traditional, conservative approach which says that the Gospels[33] offer a historically reliable representation of Son of Man as Jesus used it. Thus, Jesus regularly employed this turn of phrase to speak about his present condition, impending death and resurrection, and coming glory. While the relationship between Daniel 7 and messianic predictions may not have had any contemporary consensus and may not even have existed, Jesus is certainly able to have made those connections himself. Only towards the end of his ministry did he make it clear that he was drawing on the vision of Daniel 7, but nonetheless he was using it as a title for himself all along. This view fits into the so-called "Messianic secret" as Jesus rejects more obvious titles such as "Christ" and "Son of God" but willingly calls himself Son of Man which he can fill out with his own interpretation. This view has the great advantage of simplicity—taking the Gospels as whole volumes of historical narrative results in a more straightforward task of reading what is there. Questions of the veracity of such an approach will be dealt with below (esp. ch. 2). The inherent simplicity of such an approach does not, however, excuse the overly simplistic exegesis

---

31. Burkett, *Son of Man Debate*, 123.

32. See, for example, the discussion of implied and actual readers in Bolt, *Jesus' Defeat of Death*, ch. 1, esp. 1–10.

33. Or at least the Synoptic Gospels do.

that is sometimes associated with conservative presentations on the topic of Son of Man. The exegetical puzzles and questions of linguistic and thematic background sources remain. Why, for example, if the phrase was a title used by Jesus himself, even though only recently coined, would it not be used in the Pauline Epistles or even in the sermons found in Acts? Jesus certainly had no hesitation in using it, even apparently where people were confused by his use of it (e.g. John 12:34). Secondly, this view gives little direction on the question of background beyond Daniel.

Can There Be an Overlapping Solution?

Though these positions are generally exclusive to one another, there may be at least one middleway. Müller, who takes an idiomatic interpretation, almost offers such a path when he writes in his conclusion:

> In the Gospels it is employed by the Jesus figure as a clear self-reference. Its only apparent messianic content does not come from the expression itself as if it were a title, but from what is said about the Son of man exposing the christology of the individual gospels. . . . Although a more or less colourless circumlocution in its origin, in the Gospels it gained a certain content through its placement in the construction of the story of the earthly Jesus as the Messiah. . . . We cannot trace the expression Son of man back before its emergence in the Gospel of Mark. Even if it has its roots in Aramaic circumlocution, it has been transformed (perhaps also, through translation) with new meaning. The authors of the later Gospels took it over, either directly from the Gospel of Mark, or—what can only be a hypothesis—from sources behind Mark.[34]

If this last hypothesis is correct, moreover if those sources behind Mark accurately represent Jesus's own mannerism in using the phrase, then there happens to be a large overlap between the circumlocution idiom theory and the conservative position. That is, Jesus himself, by regular usage in important phrases about his current and future role may have made a circumlocution so much his own that the record of his speech would seem awkward if it were placed on the lips of someone else.

An analogy may be drawn at this point to Australian Rugby League player and professional boxer Anthony Mundine. His consistent self-reference as "The Man," and the reporting of that in local media, has meant that many Australians would recognize his voice in the quote, "I'm going

---

34. Müller, *Expression Son of Man*, 418–19.

to show you why I'm called 'The Man.'"[35] Thus in context what would have previously been a simple reference to a particular man, is easily recognized as an idiom for "the boss" and has a particular exclusive reference to Mundine. While often placed between inverted commas, to remove any doubt, it would be confusing if in an article about Mundine anyone else was referred to as the man (though this would be entirely legitimate in another context), and such confusion would be amplified in a verbal rather than literary context. Is it possible that, in a similar way, Jesus used "son of man" in whatever language it was first used, in such a particular manner that his disciples understood it to be some special exclusive self-reference?

Adopting such a view may go a long way in explaining the historical problem raised above—why Jesus is rarely called Son of Man outside of the Gospels. Since Paul was not a follower of the earthly Jesus, he is unlikely to have ever heard this peculiar speech mannerism and so would have been less likely to use it.[36] Moreover, the other New Testament writers may have associated the phrase so closely with the voice of Jesus that they did not think to use it except in quoting him directly as they do throughout the Gospels. Such a position is just as open to criticism as any other yet put forward, perhaps doubly so since it combines elements of two positions put forward above, but it may offer some attractive and intriguing solutions to the Son of Man issue.

The Contribution of This Book to the Scholarship

Over twenty-five years ago, Reginald Fuller noted that "[t]he problem of the Son of Man is a can of worms. No one can write anything about it which will command general assent or provide a definitive solution."[37] This remains a fair representation of the situation in modern New Testament scholarship. Dale Allison correctly identifies one of the major reasons: "My guess is that most New Testament scholars form a fairly clear picture of Jesus near the start of their careers, a picture that, while it may undergo some modification in subsequent years, rarely loses its basic features. Once a paradigm about Jesus is in place, a cognitive basis will also be in place."[38] Therefore, this thesis should hardly be considered as offering some conclusive statement on the Son of Man, and what conclusions may be drawn are made humbly and are

---

35. Cited in Fox Sports, "Anthony Mundine."

36. While Porter's recent work has raised some questions it seems highly unlikely that Paul had sustained interaction with the earthly Jesus. Porter, *When Paul Met Jesus*.

37. Fuller, "Die Entchristologisierung," 721.

38. Allison, *Historical Christ*, 59.

open to reexamination. The purpose of this book is to discern the meaning of ὁ υἱὸς τοῦ ἀνθρώπου in Mark's Gospel and to determine whether, contrary to the general perception in scholarship, the book of the prophet Ezekiel may offer some background for this phrase and explore its implications.

Having begun with the preceding brief examination of the state of play of Son of Man scholarship, this thesis will discuss an alternative order of argument to that taken and proceed to establish an exegetical methodology for considering the Son of Man sayings in Mark's Gospel, as well as comment on the integrity of such an approach for reliable historical information about Jesus (ch. 2). It will then work according to this methodology to establish what should be understood by Jesus's use of Son of Man in Mark's Gospel (ch. 3) and draw from that work overall conclusions about the themes and unifying concepts (ch. 4). After establishing some understanding of the Markan Son of Man, the question "Why explore Ezekiel for background?" will be answered (ch. 5). Then a profile of Ezekiel's בֶּן־אָדָם will be set out (ch. 6) and compared to the Son of Man found in Mark (ch. 7). Before its conclusion (ch. 9), a chapter will discuss the veracity and wider ramifications of this comparison (ch. 8).

2

Methodological Questions

An Alternative Order of Argument

It would have been possible to answer questions related to this topic in a completely reverse way to that set out in this book. That is, in order to examine how the sons of man in Ezekiel and Mark compare, rather than beginning with Mark and then moving to Ezekiel, an argument could begin in Ezekiel and then move to Mark. This alternative would likewise examine the main contours of Son of Man scholarship, but it would then move on to raising issues with regard to the suitability or completeness of the Danielic background for some aspects of the denotation and connotations associated with Son of Man. It could then have explored Ezekiel's בֶּן־אָדָם and established what concepts and themes are associated with it before turning to Mark to examine each instance of a Son of Man saying and whether they might be better understood assuming some Ezekielic influence. At one level this might allow a simpler answer to the question of whether Ezekiel might offer some background for the Son of Man in Mark, but this alternative route was not taken for three reasons. The first is practical—the book generally presents the material in the order in which it was researched and written. The second is methodological—it is well known that a researcher will find themes and possible background when they go looking for them. In contrast, the argumentation chosen should allow Mark to speak for itself before Ezekiel is examined and comparisons made. The third reason is that the chosen method allows for some examination of issues slightly wider than those which the question must answer. Most important among these wider issues is the attempt to find overarching themes and concepts related to Son of Man in Mark's Gospel. This is not to say that a thesis presenting an argument that went from Ezekiel to Mark would necessarily be short-circuited or shortsighted, but the method chosen means that the possibility of such problems (or perhaps just the appearance of them) is mitigated. Done properly, both the chosen course of argument and this alternative should lead to similar conclusions.

Justification for the Exegetical Approach Taken

At one level this book could take the view that it is seeking to find Mark's particular presentation of the Son of Man and thus justify its methodology rather simply: the text called the Gospel of Mark is one single coherent narrative intended to convey the significant news of Jesus Christ (Mark 1:1) and while "external factors remain relevant," any phrases used of Jesus will receive "their most decisive imprint from the literary strategy and the literary world which hosts them . . . their narrative foreground rather than their historical background."[1] As a whole, Mark's story hinges on the confession of Jesus as the Christ in 8:29. The use of geographical settings in the book is very pronounced as the action begins with John baptizing Jesus in the Jordan, moves around Galilee as Jesus begins his ministry, on to the vicinity of Tyre and Sidon, before coming back south around Galilee. The action then moves north again toward Caesarea Philippi for the confession and transfiguration, and then south to Jerusalem where Jesus will die. Thus, it makes sense for a full understanding of the Markan Son of Man not to isolate the Son of Man sayings, but to consider them within their episodes with an eye to the wider narrative of the book and to determine the Son of Man concept that emerges through the Gospel. This is what shall be attempted in chapter 3, while chapter 4 will offer a synthesis of this exegetical work.

Of course, it would be fair to question whether this is a reasonable approach for gaining an appreciation of the historical Jesus and the phrase Son of Man and its origins. Maurice Casey's approach would lead one to conclude it does not. Based on his view that the underlying Aramaic בר אנשא is only a circumlocution which can take a "general and specific level of meaning,"[2] the only sayings found in Mark that Casey admits as authentic to the context "in which they are now found" are 2:28, 9:12, 10:45, and 14:21, while Mark 3:28–29 demonstrates an alternative translation of an underlying Aramaic source common to Matthew 12:32/Luke 12:10.[3] Those

---

1. Broadhead, *Naming Jesus*, 29.
2. Casey, *Solution*, 314.
3. Casey, *Solution*, 143.

admitted still receive some significant reinterpretation in comparison with traditional scholarship, while some not admitted are reevaluated by Casey to see what their original setting and meaning might have been. Thus, while largely undiscernible to a Greek reader, Mark 2:10, 8:31, 8:38, and 10:45 might have originally been general maxims about God giving some people the power to deal with psychosomatic illnesses (2:10), the goodness of the life of service (10:45), inevitable death and general resurrection (8:31), and the role of humanity in the final judgment (8:38).[4] Since they can only understand Jesus's use of the phrase as exclusive and might demonstrate dependence on an expected "son of man" figure from Daniel 7:13, Mark 13:26 and 14:62 are entirely implausible as genuine sayings.[5] An alternative view can be found in both Burkett and Müller. Though the former reads the origins of Son of Man as a title arising from Daniel 7 and the latter as a circumlocution, both argue that the New Testament Gospels largely represent the interpretation of the church soon after Jesus's death, yet both also leave open the possibility that the origins of the phrase might go back to Jesus.[6] Burkett writes, "[t]he church's language about Jesus has been retrojected onto the lips of Jesus himself,"[7] but adds "[e]ven if it were certain, however, that all of the Son of Man sayings originated in the early church, we could not be certain about the title 'Son of Man' itself. The title may well have existed prior to any of the sayings in which it appears. If so, we would have no way of tracing the title to its point of origin in the Christian tradition. Its origin would lie beyond the horizon of our vision."[8] Müller similarly concludes, "the expression takes its meaning from contemporary christological thinking ... the outcome of the interpretative efforts of the community" and adds, "we cannot trace the expression Son of man back before its emergence in the Gospel of Mark."[9] Though he concedes "some sort of continuity [with the historical Jesus] is certainly a possibility" he is confident that "the expression does not have any special meaning before it receives it through its concrete context in the respective Gospels."[10]

The concern with Casey's idiom approach has been discussed above, but on this specific issue of the authenticity of the majority of the sayings

---

4. Casey, *Solution*, 116–211, esp. 165, 202–3, 205–6, 185, 132.

5. Casey, *Solution*, 242–44.

6. See respectively: Burkett, *Son of Man Debate*, 121–24; Müller, *Expression Son of Man*, 417–19.

7. Burkett, *Son of Man Debate*, 123.

8. Burkett, *Son of Man Debate*, 124.

9. Müller, *Expression Son of Man*, 419.

10. Müller, *Expression Son of Man*, 419.

one must ask, in a similar vein to Owen:[11] Why would the early church have bothered to preserve mundane general maxims? How did they come to be modified so much and so quickly? Is it really impossible that Jesus could have drawn on Daniel 7 to convey something of his self-understanding? And why, if Jesus's original sayings were so much less dramatic, would he have caused so much controversy, and be accused of, and then condemned for, blasphemy?

In response to Burkett's and Müller's concerns, it must be admitted that exactly how the sources of the Gospels came together cannot finally be discerned. It would not be unreasonable however to take seriously the dichotomy proposed by Freyne: "Either we accept that the early followers of Jesus had some interest in and memory of the historical figure of Jesus as they began to proclaim the good news about him, or we must abandon the [historical] process entirely."[12] Then it would not be difficult to conclude that the Gospel authors "were not creators of the tradition but custodians,"[13] who "did not wildly invent material [but they] developed it, shaped it, and directed it in the ways they wished,"[14] and that the plans, "dreams, ideas, symbols, and terms" they inherited had come from Jesus himself.[15] With the exception of its conclusion (i.e. whatever can be said to follow 16:8), which is not relevant to this Son of Man question, the antiquity and manuscript consistency of the Gospel of Mark is well attested and its priority among the Gospels has been widely accepted. Thus, without resolving the text's ultimate credibility, which in any case appears to be beyond academic enquiry, proper consideration of Mark's Gospel may bring a reader to the very limit of what can be known about both Jesus and the Son of Man.[16]

In the next chapter, each of Mark's Son of Man sayings will be considered under three headings, firstly the scene in which the saying comes, secondly the wording of the saying itself, and thirdly the emerging picture of the Son of Man in the narrative of Mark's story. This *exegetical-narratival* approach will allow a clear understanding of the Markan Son of Man to be presented in chapter 4.[17] Assuming Markan priority, this will also be the

---

11. Owen, "Problems," esp. 45–46.
12. Freyne, *Jesus*, 4.
13. McClymond, *Familiar Stranger*, 43.
14. Sanders, *Historical Figure*, 193.
15. Charlesworth, *Jesus within Judaism*, 167.
16. Crossley recently argued for Mark's composition to have occurred between the midthirties to the midforties. Crossley, *Date of Mark's Gospel*, 206–9.
17. It should be noted here that since this approach adopts a historical view of the text, and will read it as a coherent single narrative, there may not be the kind of smooth, unified themes that one might expect with, say, a work of fiction. That is, while the text

earliest possible understanding of ὁ υἱὸς τοῦ ἀνθρώπου, and the best possible chance of gaining an authentic understanding of Jesus's own presentation of the issue.

---

can be understood as a collection of selected and curated episodes of the life of Jesus, shaped by the final Gospel redactor (whom history names as Mark), if it records actual events, then one would expect some incongruous, incomplete, and pendent ideas, themes and events, since all accurate recording of history must represent the variegated happenstance of reality.

3

The Son of Man in Mark

Mark 2:1–12

The Scene (2:1–12)

MARK'S NARRATIVE RETURNS TO Capernaum in 2:1 with Jesus in a house, most likely Peter's (cf. 1:29).[1] The problem of Jesus's popularity (1:45) becomes apparent in 2:1–2 where the house is so full of people that they spill out of the door. As in 1:32–33, Jesus is sought for miraculous healing, but this time only one person is mentioned, a paralyzed man brought by four others (2:3). Unable to reach Jesus due to the crowd they take the drastic, though reasonably straightforward, action of digging through what was most likely a thatch and clay roof.[2] Jesus clearly approves of such deep desire to reach him, yet rather than fulfill their expectation of healing, he says to the paralytic, Τέκνον, ἀφίενταί σου αἱ ἁμαρτίαι.

Surprising as this may have been for the five companions, the narrative's concern lies with the shock of the scribes who were present. δέ and imperfect tense forms are used to mark this narrative development and move offline to the main narrative, their introduction and concern regarding Jesus's absolution (2:6–7).[3] To this point in Mark's Gospel, Jesus was

---

1. Marcus, *Mark 1–8*, 215; Edwards, *Gospel*; France, *Gospel of Mark*, 122; Van Iersel, *Mark*, 145–46; Stein notes the possibility, but also suggests that it may just be a house (cf. 7:24, 9:28) or perhaps Jesus's home (cf. e.g. Matt 4:13 and possibly Mark 2:15, 3:20), Stein, *Mark*, 116.

2. McCown, "Luke's Translation," 213–16.

3. For this interpretation of δέ see Runge, *Discourse Grammar*, 28–36. For this

contrasted with the scribes in regard to authority by the crowd (1:27), but in the episode preceding this one, Jesus adheres to Mosaic traditions (1:44).[4] Here Jesus's contrast with scribes is both direct and, given the scribes' expertise in Torah requirements for forgiveness and absolution, sharp.[5] Since Jesus infringes on an exclusively "divine prerogative" he is considered blasphemous.[6]

Jesus, aware of their offence at his declaration, uses this first Son of Man saying to counter their understanding of how forgiveness is declared. Jesus proves his authority to forgive through performing another impossible task, namely, also making the paralytic physically well.[7] Verse 12 shows the outcome—the paralytic walks, everyone is shocked (ἐξίστασθαι), and they glorify God. Since the action changes location to Lake Galilee in verse 13, verse 12 is the end of this first of five units set in Capernaum (the others being 2:13–17; 18–22; 23–28; 3:1–6).[8]

The Saying (2:8b–11)

The saying itself is disjointed since Jesus begins speaking to the scribes in verse 8 and then switches to the paralytic in verse 11, but the thought is singular: Jesus has authority both to forgive and to heal. It begins as Jesus counters the internal questions of the scribes with a spoken challenge and rather difficult question of his own. Τί ταῦτα διαλογίζεσθε ἐν ταῖς καρδίαις ὑμῶν; τί ἐστιν εὐκοπώτερον, εἰπεῖν τῷ παραλυτικῷ, Ἀφίενταί σου αἱ ἁμαρτίαι, ἢ εἰπεῖν, "Ἔγειρε καὶ ἆρον τὸν κράβαττόν σου καὶ περιπάτει; France suggests that the correct "answer to Jesus' rhetorical question must therefore be that it is εὐκοπώτερον to say 'Your sins are forgiven,' since that is the point to be proved (v. 10)."[9] As Edwards points out, "From a human perspective it is safe to pronounce the forgiveness of sins, since that statement cannot be falsified."[10] Neither however, is actually "easier," since both are impos-

---

understanding of imperfect tense forms see Campbell, *Indicative Mood*, 77–102.

4. Culpepper suggests that ch. 1 spoke of Jesus's conflict with spiritual powers, but, returning to Capernaum, he will be in conflict with religious powers. Culpepper, *Mark*, 73. Focant calls the section, "Galilean controversy" and examines a possible chiastic structure of 2:1—3:6. Focant, *According to Mark*, 86–88.

5. So Edwards, *Gospel*, 77; Dunn, *Jesus, Paul and the Law*, 27.

6. France, *Gospel of Mark*, 126; so also, Culpepper, *Mark*, 79.

7. Hooker, *Son of Man*, 84–86; Marcus, *Mark 1–8*, 223–24; Culpepper, *Mark*, 78–79.

8. Witherington, *Gospel of Mark*, 109–11.

9. France, *Gospel of Mark*, 127.

10. Edwards, *Gospel*, 79; so also, Marcus, *Mark 1–8*, 217–18; Stein, *Mark*, 120;

sible. Human words alone could change neither the paralytic's ability to stand physically before the people in that room nor spiritually before God in judgment.[11]

Leaving the question of ability (δύναμαι, v. 6) hanging, Jesus makes a direct statement about authority (ἐξουσία, v. 10) to the scribes as he deploys this first Son of Man utterance in the Gospel: ἵνα δὲ εἰδῆτε ὅτι ἐξουσίαν ἔχει ὁ υἱὸς τοῦ ἀνθρώπου ἀφιέναι ἁμαρτίας ἐπὶ τῆς γῆς—λέγει τῷ παραλυτικῷ, Σοὶ λέγω, ἔγειρε ἆρον τὸν κράβαττόν σου καὶ ὕπαγε εἰς τὸν οἶκόν σου.

δὲ marks the development between Jesus's question and his own direct statements.[12] The ἵνα marks the first clause as the purpose for the statement that Jesus is about to make to the paralytic. That is, Jesus will physically heal the man to make them know the Son of Man's authority to "heal" him of his sins (cf. 17).[13] Jesus's emphatic "σοὶ λέγω" makes plain that he is referring exclusively to himself as the Son of Man, though in context this is never in doubt.

There is a possibility that this saying alludes to Daniel 7:13–14. Both use Son of Man type language and speak of him having authority on the earth.[14] Though Daniel's setting is quite different—being apocalyptic and eschatological—that distinction in setting might be why Jesus specifies and displays a *present* and *earth-based* authority.[15] Mark's use of the passive in verse 12a might even be seeking to maintain a close union between Jesus and God, with Jesus as the divine agent without compromising the uniqueness of God.[16] As Mark's narrative continues, there will be clear allusions made to Daniel 7, and it is probably better not to assume too much is intended now and allow that relationship to be revealed and then draw conclusions once this link is more apparent.[17]

Focant, *According to Mark*, 94.

11. Cf. Culpepper, *Mark*, 80.

12. The voice of the narrator does not interrupt Jesus until λέγει τῷ παραλυτικῷ·. There is a minority view that holds that the parenthetic comment starts at v. 10. However, it would be unique in Mark for the narrator to address the reader so directly and would distance Jesus from the Son of Man phrase that is so related to his direct teaching everywhere else. Stein, *Mark*, 120–21; Guelich, *Mark 1–8:26*, 88–91; Strauss, *Mark*, 122–23; Focant, *According to Mark*, 96; contra Van Iersel, *Mark*, 149, esp. n.; Hooker, *Commentary*, 87; Hooker, *Son of Man*, 85; Lane, *Gospel of Mark*, 96–97; Witherington, *Gospel of Mark*, 116–17.

13. Cf. Stein, *Mark*, 120–21.

14. It should be noted that Psalm 8 also has a son of man with authority on earth. This is also suggested by Collins, *Mark*, 186–87.

15. Evans, *Mark 8:27—16:20*, 202–3; so also, Culpepper, *Mark*, 81.

16. Marcus, *Mark 1–8*, 224.

17. As Collins says, the allusion to Daniel "is, in effect, a riddle." Collins, *Mark*, 187.

The Emerging Picture of the Son of Man (2:1–12)

Mark's narrative offers no explanation with this first use of Son of Man, nor will it. That could mean that there was an expectation that his readers would already be familiar with the phrase through prior teaching (which could be from some combination of the Hebrew Scriptures or Gospel oral tradition). Novice readers, however, might simply have expected to learn more about this phrase as the story continues.[18] Isolated from its context in Mark's story, it would be possible to interpret the saying itself as a generic statement about the authority of humanity to declare absolution of sins (or even offer the forgiveness itself). In Mark's story however, linked so intimately with Jesus's unique authority over physical conditions, it must be understood as exclusively self-referring. That is, Jesus used this self-referential phrase to announce his present authority over physical and spiritual conditions of humanity with this paralytic as a case in point. This places Jesus above the Torah and upon God's own judgment seat. While Jesus effectively claims this authority in verse 5, in declaring the sins forgiven, the phrase Son of Man only comes after Jesus is accused of blasphemy by the scribes. Confrontation with scribes (and later, other leaders) will build from this point in the narrative and culminate in the formal charge of blasphemy after Jesus's final use of Son of Man (Mark 14:63–65). The words of the saying itself are powerful, causing a miraculous healing which staggers the whole crowd, leading them to glorify God.

Mark 2:23–28

The Scene (2:23–28)

The "scribes" in 2:1–12 were unspecified, but from that point, Mark has specified a conflict between Jesus and the Pharisaic school. In 2:13–17 Jesus countered "scribes of the Pharisees." In 2:18–22, the distinction in practice between Jesus's disciples and those of the Pharisees and John the Baptist regarding fasting is discussed. In the episode to come, Jesus will address the issue of his own action on the Sabbath (3:1–6, which brings the Capernaum setting to a close as Jesus withdraws to the sea). This episode likewise presents conflict with the Pharisees and brings together the preceding issue of eating habits with the subsequent issue of a Sabbath.[19] Just as his disciples

---

18. As Moloney writes, "Only later in the story will the full significance become clear . . . only then will the reader be made aware why this Son of Man has authority on earth." Moloney, *Gospel of Mark*, 62–63.

19. Focant notices the link backward to defending disciples and forward to the

ate when others fasted, now they pick grain (2:23, almost certainly to eat, since hunger and eating dominate vv. 25–26) and the Pharisees take offence because they themselves would not do such a thing on the Sabbath (v. 24).

Sabbath rest was considered, along with circumcision, a primary religious and cultural marker for contemporary Jews (Exod 20:8–11; Deut 5:12–15). The understanding of what was specifically proscribed in the direction "do no work" was still under discussion as evidenced by writings both before and after the first century.[20] Gathering food for meals had long been understood as forbidden (Exod 16:22–30; 34:21) so the Pharisees question Jesus about the seemingly lax attitude of his disciples. Jesus, however, not only allowed his disciples to act without discussion (vv. 23–24), but he also sets the whole debate aside by a long rhetorical question which appeals to an obscure Davidic episode (vv. 25–26, cf. 1 Sam 21:1–9).

David ate bread intended for priests (cf. Lev 24:5–9) when he and his companions were in need. While Jesus's allusion contains a problematic reference to Abiathar,[21] it is very much centered on David's action and authority. "Jesus, however, does not raise the incident in order to plead for a Sabbath exception for his hungry disciples," says Edwards. "He cites David's violation of the Torah not as an excuse for his action but as a precedent."[22] France concurs, "The focus of the scriptural allusion is not therefore so much on what David did, as on the fact that it was David who did it, and that Scripture records his act, illegal as it was, with apparent approval. The logic of Jesus' argument therefore implies a covert claim to a personal authority at least as great as that of David."[23]

The Saying (2:27–28)

Verse 27 begins with what Runge describes as a "redundant quotative frame"—καὶ ἔλεγεν αὐτοῖς—intended to highlight what follows within its context.[24] The effect is that having had Jesus build his case for a different in-

---

Sabbath. Focant, *According to Mark*, 112.

20. 1 Macc 2:29–41; Jub 2:18–33; 50:6–13; CD 10:14—11:18, m. Šabb. 7:2–4. Schürer, *History of the Jewish People*, 467–75.

21. For a concise summary of this issue, see Marcus, *Mark 1-8*, 241–42.

22. Edwards, *Gospel*, 96.

23. France, *Gospel of Mark*, 145; so also Collins, *Mark*, 205.

24. Runge, *Discourse Grammar*, 157; for discussion of Mark's use of this phrase and its implications in this context see Guelich, *Mark 1–8:26*, 123–24, 205; Gundry, *Mark*, 142–43.

terpretation, Mark draws attention to what his interpretation is. It concludes with his use of Son of Man.

First Jesus gives his understanding of how Sabbath rules should apply: Τὸ σάββατον διὰ τὸν ἄνθρωπον ἐγένετο καὶ οὐχ ὁ ἄνθρωπος διὰ τὸ σάββατον. Jesus maintains a sense of obligation to the Sabbath rest, but gives primacy to human life in its observance. The Sabbath enforces rest, but not burdens. To paraphrase Jesus, "The Sabbath exists to ensure people rest. People don't exist to ensure rest on the Sabbath." While it may have been controversial, such an interpretation was not entirely foreign to Judaism, for one Rabbi would later write, "The Sabbath has been given to you; you have not been given to the Sabbath."[25]

This understanding of the Sabbath means that it was legitimate to pick up a snack as you walked along without considering it "work," but it also brings a more startling result. Verse 28 begins with a resultant clause marked by ὥστε with an indicative (ἐστιν). κύριος is placed emphatically early in the sentence, as though it offers an answer to the question, "Who is the Lord of the Sabbath?"[26] The answer is ὁ υἱὸς τοῦ ἀνθρώπου. The nature of this lordship though, is a matter of some discussion. France, for example, concludes that here κύριος functions "in the normal lexical sense of the one who is in a position of superior authority"[27] but Edwards believes that this is much more a claim for divine authority.[28]

The use of καί following ὥστε, where it is not functioning to mark a new clause or list, is not common in the New Testament (the other examples include: Matt 24:24; Acts 19:12; Rom 7:4; 2 Cor 1:8; Gal 2:13; and 1 Pet 4:19). In such instances it always appears to be linking a substantive with some aforementioned concept or entity, and the English word "likewise" offers a suitable and broad enough gloss in such cases. Thus, καί could be understood as functioning in a kind of ascensive way—expressing a "final addition or point of focus"[29]—but doing so in comparison to an earlier concept, or it could be understood to function adverbially in a comparative way. What is not clear, however, is what the ὁ υἱὸς τοῦ ἀνθρώπου or his lordship is being compared to.

One possibility is that καί is intended to join ὁ υἱὸς τοῦ ἀνθρώπου to the ἄνθρωπος of verse 27, treating the terms as poetic synonyms (cf. Ps 8:4), such

---

25. Mek. Exod 31:13. It represents, "a line of thought already present within Judaism." Moloney, *Gospel of Mark*, 69.

26. Edwards, *Gospel*, 97; Runge, *Discourse Grammar*, 181–205.

27. France, *Gospel of Mark*, 148.

28. Edwards, *Gospel*, 97.

29. Wallace, *Greek Grammar*, 670, italics removed.

that Jesus could be saying, "The Sabbath was made for man, so likewise a human is lord of the Sabbath." However, such a general interpretation does not work well elsewhere in Mark (this would be the only place where a general application could work in its immediate context). France therefore concludes that it is "inconceivable that Mark could have intended, or expected his readers to understand, a different sense for the phrase in this case" and since neither Matthew nor Luke include the content of verse 27 they clearly understood that Jesus, and no-one else, is "Son of Man."[30] Moreover, the preceding and subsequent episodes are focusing on Jesus's interpretations and authority, and, within this episode, Jesus is building his exclusive authority by comparing himself to David, while a generic interpretation would give all humans a broad authority over the Sabbath. Collins may be right in suggesting that the saying has a "play on words" and "riddle": initially a generic sense can be entertained, but the solution is to see "that 'the son of man' is 'the Son of Man.'"[31]

Another possibility is that καί joins ὁ υἱὸς τοῦ ἀνθρώπου to the ἄνθρωπος, but is indicating an assumed sense of general lordship over humanity.[32] "The Sabbath was made for man, so the Son of Man (who rules humans) is also lord of the Sabbath." Similar to this it could be linking τοῦ σαββάτου with some implied authority in the previous verse: ". . . so the Son of Man is lord of the Sabbath (as the rest of humanity is)." Either would sit well with the relationship established between Jesus and David and their respective companions/disciples (vv. 23–27). The former would give some leeway to people over their Sabbath, but place the ultimate authority on Jesus for a decision, while the latter appears to give too much away in regard to loosing the Sabbath according to personal preference.[33] While the former of these two interpretations is therefore to be preferred, it would depend on some preexisting understanding of Son of Man at the time of Jesus for it to be readily understood in its context.

Instead, καί could be intended to relate that there is another who is Lord of the Sabbath, that is God, who is the agent of the divine passives in verse 27. The idea of naming a "Lord of the Sabbath" who is not simply God would shock any contemporary Jewish audience, let alone a devout

---

30. France, *Gospel of Mark*, 147. So also, Marcus, *Mark 1–8*, 246; Stein, *Mark*, 149; Focant, *According to Mark*, 114; Van Iersel, *Mark*, 159.

31. Collins, *Mark*, 204–5.

32. Stein, *Mark*, 149–50.

33. "If 2:27 is understood in the very liberal sense of a lordship of human beings over the Sabbath, there is . . . no reason to affirm that someone such as the Son of Man is its Lord. 2:28 would therefore translate a christological incomprehension of 2:27." Focant, *According to Mark*, 116–17; following Bartelmus, "Mk 2,27," 62.

Pharisaic one (cf. Exod 16:25; 20:10; Lev 19:3, 30; Deut 5:14, Ezek 20:12–13) and κύριος is almost always used of God in Mark's Gospel.[34] Edwards concludes that "God, as we noted earlier, had instituted the Sabbath (Gen 2:3), and Jesus now presumes preeminence over it! Once again Jesus puts himself squarely in the place of God." Edwards may be too strong in his phrasing, but Jesus's obscure phrasing certainly allows Mark's readers to infer an intentional claim beyond any Davidic-Messianic expectation.

The Emerging Picture of the Son of Man (2:23–28)

As in Mark 2:1–12, Jesus uses Son of Man to refer to himself in a serious claim of authority, this time over the Sabbath.[35] This leads to four wider implications for Jesus's authority. Firstly, the Son of Man has authority over the Sabbath because it was made for humans. Why this should be is not explained in these verses. It may be something inherent to the natures of Sabbath, humanity, and Son of Man and may have some relation to the following points which apply in any case. So, this indicates that the Son of Man is able to determine the proper actions for humans at least in regard to the Sabbath. Secondly, this text shows that the Son of Man has authority over Torah interpretation. This extends beyond Sabbath since, read in the wider context, Jesus and the Pharisaic school are contrasted on issues such as contamination by sinners and fasting. Jesus's precedent in David also relates to a wider issue than Sabbath regulation. The Son of Man is Lord of the Sabbath, and the rest of the Torah with it.[36] Thirdly, Jesus establishes a link between himself as Son of Man, and a messianic hope,[37] and yet, while he points to David as precedent, he surpasses David's claim to authority. Indeed, fourthly, whether it is wrapped up in the word κύριος or not, Jesus claimed something approaching a divine authority due to his status as ὁ υἱὸς τοῦ ἀνθρώπου during his ministry.

Additionally, as in Mark 2:1–12, there is a clear sense that the Son of Man is in conflict with the leadership of the Jewish people. In comparison to Mark 2:1–12, the conflict is more intense and specified as being with the Pharisaic school (rather than undefined "scribes"). While the Pharisees do not respond to Jesus in this episode, they do so in the next one, which

---

34. Mark 12:36–37 seems to be the only place that κύριος is used as a christological title.

35. So also, Moloney, *Gospel of Mark*, 69.

36. Focant reaches the same conclusion. Focant, *According to Mark*, 114.

37. Marcus writes on these verses, "for Mark the Davidic Messiah and the Danielic Son of Man are one and the same, and their name is Jesus." Marcus, *Mark 1–8*, 246.

concludes the wider unit begun at 2:1. In 3:1–6, Jesus will act out an authority over the Sabbath, which results in religious and political leaders who would not usually agree being united in their desire to kill Jesus. Both Son of Man sayings in chapter 2 arise in contexts of conflict with scribes and Pharisees, and the latter leads to an episode where they seek his death.

Mark 8:27—9:1

The Setting (8:27—9:1)

This scene contains two Son of Man sayings, one toward the start and one at the end (vv. 31, 38).[38] The events take place as Jesus and his disciples head toward Caesarea Philippi, in the far north of the Jewish region. Mark's theme of Jesus's identity is addressed directly by Jesus's questions.[39] Just as they will turn back south towards Jerusalem geographically, so too Mark's narrative, his εὐαγγέλιον Ἰησοῦ Χριστοῦ (1:1), reaches a turning point: while the people remain confused about Jesus's identity (8:27-28), Peter, on behalf of the disciples, now recognizes Jesus as ὁ χριστός (v. 29), so the teaching of Jesus and the themes of Mark's narrative shift in focus.[40]

The Son of Man sayings arise as Jesus warns and exchanges rebukes with his disciples—Peter in particular. The lofty recognition of Jesus as Messiah is met with a warning not to tell others.[41] Why Jesus desired concealment of such information has long been debated,[42] but Jesus continues on to speak about the situation about to be faced by the Son of Man (the first saying to be looked at below).[43] Peter responds to Jesus's warning and teach-

---

38. Though there may be a place to discuss Markan redaction of this section, the unity of the story as it appears is observable through the lack of temporal and spatial changes. The crowd's involvement from v. 34 is new but it comes partly as a direct response to Peter's attempt at a quiet rebuke of Jesus before his teaching about suffering is spread. On the unity of the episode see: Collins, *Mark*, 407; Gundry, *Mark*, 425; for discussion of the possible underlying sources see: Stein, *Mark*, 395–97.

39. Collins, *Mark*, 401.

40. Moloney, *Gospel of Mark*, 167–72; Collins, *Mark*, 398.

41. This matches Jesus's earlier directions to demons (1:34; 3:11–12), but note that he is less concerned in 5:7, 19. Collins, *Mark*, 402.

42. As Garland notes, Wrede's *Messianic Secret* "vexed Markan scholarship for decades," but there is a growing view that the secrecy found in Mark's Gospel simply reflects the historical Jesus and the setting of the final form of the Gospel. Wrede, *Messianic Secret*; Garland, *Theology of Mark's Gospel*, 368–87; Watson, *Honor among Christians*; Räisänen, *Messianic Secret*.

43. Since Mark affirms Jesus as Christ in 1:1, Jesus's command to silence, however else it may be understood, cannot be an indication of error in the confession as it

ing with a rebuke of his own (8:32). Jesus then rebukes Peter in the strongest terms (8:33) and calls his disciples and the crowd to hear the teaching that Peter tried to conceal. This speech concludes with the second Son of Man saying in this scene (8:34—9:1).

The Saying (8:31–32)

The content of the saying is presented in indirect speech, but that the content came directly from Jesus is made clear in verse 32[44]—Jesus spoke about this plainly (παρρησία). The comment that Jesus ἤρξατο διδάσκειν and the use of indirect speech indicate that this was a new phase of teaching[45]—the construction used conveys an ingressive *Aktionsart*.[46] It is core information to which Jesus will return (and Mark records only a few examples of this happening in later sayings). Both Peter's rebuke and Jesus's subsequent response, where he refers to an expectation of execution for himself (ἀράτω τὸν σταυρὸν αὐτοῦ καὶ ἀκολουθείτω μοι), indicate Jesus should be understood as speaking about himself as the Son of Man.

Jesus's confidence is surprising since he speaks of the Son of Man's impending and necessary deep[47] suffering, rejection by the elders, chief priests and scribes, and death. Elders were the traditional leaders and the senior members of prominent families, scribes were educated leaders, and placed with the chief priests this group can be identified with the Sanhedrin.[48] Though the manner of the death is not yet spelled out, Jesus would readily be understood as speaking of a formal rejection—a condemnation—of him and his ministry, resulting in his death.[49] Though it is not stated, the

---

stands. Stein, *Mark*, 399.

44. The particular language used (namely, the order of those rejecting Jesus; the lack of reference to crucifixion; and the use of ἀνίστημι) indicates that this is unlikely to be a Markan invention, since it does not conform to patterns found in the book. Instead this likely reflects an underlying oral source for this change of direction in Jesus's teaching. Gundry, *Mark*, 429–30.

45. France, *Gospel of Mark*, 327; Stein, *Mark*, 401; Hooker, *Commentary*, 205. As Stein points out Matthew 16:21 certainly supports this reading.

46. Campbell, *Non-Indicative Verbs*, 102–5.

47. With Gundry, I think it more likely that Mark's use of πολλά here (as in 1:45) is adverbial rather than an object of παθεῖν. Even if this assumption is incorrect, suffering many things would undoubtedly amount to great distress. Gundry, *Mark*, 429.

48. Collins, *Mark*, 404–5.

49. This text, "presumes the decision of Jesus' adversaries to kill him." Van Iersel, *Mark*, 283.

sense in which this is "necessary" must be due to a divine plan revealed in Scripture (for those with the ability to interpret it).[50]

For Peter, a disciple in a hierarchical and honor-shame culture, to attempt to rebuke his master, whom he has just confessed as Messiah, shows how jarring the content and manner of Jesus's teaching must have felt. For the readers of Mark's narrative, however, both Peter's confession and the desires of scribes and leaders to kill Jesus are somewhat expected (Mark 1:1; 3:6). Death is not the end point though, as Jesus promises a resurrection after three days (μετὰ τρεῖς ἡμέρας ἀναστῆναι), and this expectation would help explain Jesus's confidence in conveying his expectation of his fate. Jesus knows that he will rise again.

The timing of the resurrection "after three days" appears problematic since Jesus rose "on the third day." Matthew and Luke consistently use τῇ τρίτῃ ἡμέρᾳ instead (the exception being Matt 27:63–64) and Gundry points out Hosea 6:2 LXX parallels μετὰ δύο ἡμέρας with ἐν τῇ ἡμέρᾳ τῇ τρίτῃ.[51] Josephus, however, shows an event μετὰ τρεῖς ἡμέρας can be expected to occur τῇ τρίτῃ τῶν ἡμερῶν (*Ant.* 7.280 with 281; 8.214 with 218).[52] It seems likely that the "phrase used by Matthew and Luke is therefore apologetically safer"[53] in that it is clearer, but it would not be surprising for μετὰ τρεῖς ἡμέρας to be understood as referring to the day after tomorrow.

The Saying (8:38)

The resurrection vindication of verse 31 is taken much further, both in time and in degree, in the second saying of chapter 8. This saying is affected by two textual criticism issues found in the important texts of 𝔓45 and W. The first is whether λόγους should be omitted after με καὶ τοὺς ἐμούς. τοὺς ἐμοὺς λόγους would refer to Jesus's preceding teaching about his and his disciples' impending death but could extend across his wider gospel proclamation and teaching. On its own, τοὺς ἐμούς would more likely refer to Jesus's followers—"those that are mine." "If λόγους is not original, it is hard to explain its presence in such a wide variety of different types of text . . . λόγους is most likely original and was accidentally omitted because

---

50. Though scholars point to many possible passages which Jesus might have in mind, e.g. Psalm 118:22, Isaiah 53. See, for example, Collins, *Mark*, 404; Stein, *Mark*, 403–4; Gundry, *Mark*, 446–47.

51. Gundry, *Mark*, 448.

52. France, *Gospel of Mark*, 336–37.

53. France, *Gospel of Mark*, 377.

of the similarity in ending of the words ἐμοὺς and λόγους."⁵⁴ The second textual criticism concern involves reading καί instead of μετά before "the holy angels" and looks to have arisen to harmonize with Luke 9:26.⁵⁵ Even with such changes the general thrust of the passage remains unaffected: Jesus promises a coming of the Son of Man ἐν τῇ δόξῃ τοῦ πατρός and thus anyone who is offended or ashamed in the present generation is warned of a reversal in the age to come.

In response to Peter's attempted rebuke, Jesus has called the crowd to take up their cross and follow him (v. 34), explained the life-and-death stakes involved (vv. 35–37), and now explains why a failure to properly respect his path of impending suffering will be so costly. If Jesus and his words cause people to be ashamed now and thus to ignore them, then the Son of Man will be ashamed of them when he comes ἐν τῇ δόξῃ τοῦ πατρὸς αὐτοῦ μετὰ τῶν ἀγγέλων τῶν ἁγίων (Mark 8:38). The setting of the warning—ἐν τῇ γενεᾷ ταύτῃ τῇ μοιχαλίδι καὶ ἁμαρτωλῷ—sets a clear sense of ongoing conflict between Jesus and his faithful followers on the one hand and those who would deny him under persecution,⁵⁶ and thus be aligned with the adulterous⁵⁷ and sinful, on the other. "This generation" is a broad enough idea to extend from Jesus's own time of speaking to when Jesus comes ἐν τῇ δόξῃ τοῦ πατρὸς αὐτοῦ.⁵⁸ Since Jesus speaks of τοῦ πατρὸς αὐτοῦ, he equates the Son of Man with Son of God.⁵⁹ As at 2:10–11, though more likely in this case, there is a possible allusion here to Daniel's night vision.⁶⁰ This time the setting is more similar, being eschatological and apocalyptic, and the similarity of reference is in a Son of Man "coming" and being glorious and powerful like God.⁶¹

---

54. Omanson and Metzger, *Textual Guide*, 81. The minor error in accentuation is original.

55. Omanson and Metzger, *Textual Guide*, 82.

56. Stein, *Mark*, 410.

57. This word is used in its prophetic sense of failing to keep faith with God. Collins, *Mark*, 411.

58. Cf. Seccombe, *God's Kingdom*, 596–97.

59. Collins, *Mark*, 412; Stein, *Mark*, 409.

60. Marcus, *Mark 8–16*, 620, 629–30.

61. Again, however, it might be noted that Psalm 8 contains "a son of man" having glory and a status מְעַט מֵאֱלֹהִים.

The Emerging Picture of the Son of Man (8:27—9:1)

As has been seen through the last two Son of Man sayings, Son of Man is exclusively self-referring and comes from Jesus directly, even where presented indirectly. Son of Man is also again deployed in relation to conflict, with elders, chief priests and scribes in verse 31 rejecting the Son of Man prior to his suffering and death. The saying also precipitates a new conflict between Jesus and Peter. Undoing Peter's attempt at rebuke, and answering any disciples that may have felt similarly, Jesus called his followers to be willing to suffer execution for his sake and pits faithful followers against both the wider world and those who might become ashamed of and disown Jesus. While death is to be expected for Jesus and those loyal to him in this generation, the second Son of Man saying emphasizes that a reversal of fortunes will occur in a final judgment.

These Son of Man sayings differ significantly on the issue of present authority, which was so dominant in the previous two sayings. In contrast to the preceding material, the first saying here offers a grating image of the Son of Man suffering, facing rejection from Jewish leaders, and even dying. These things are "necessary" and though the resurrection mentioned offers a fairly immediate (if understated) vindication, Peter's shocked response is not difficult to understand. After all, he has just declared Jesus to be God's promised king and Jesus has only just begun to teach about this suffering and resurrection. Even so, Jesus still has authority enough to demand that the crowd follow him on this way (8:34). As Moloney observes, "These words open the second major section of the Gospel of Mark, dedicated to the story of the *crucified* Christ and Son of God, the *suffering* and *finally* vindicated Son of Man."[62]

This final vindication, and with it a strong sense of authority, comes in the second Son of Man saying. There Jesus reveals that the Son of Man, who has led his people carrying their crosses, has an "ultimate destiny" which "will reverse the scandal of his being rejected and killed."[63] This authority is however set at the end of this "generation" which does not receive Jesus and his words. At that time the Son of Man will lead the procession of God's angelic army and be involved in a judgment of people according to how they have responded to him and his words. In the eschaton, as it was in relation to sin (2:1–12) and to the Sabbath (2:23–28), the fortunes of every human are tied to the Son of Man.[64]

---

62. Moloney, *Gospel of Mark*, 167.
63. Gundry, *Mark*, 439.
64. Stein, *Mark*, 411–12.

These sayings also bring in a clear relationship between Son of Man and Christ. Jesus accepts, yet silences the talk of Christ and immediately speaks of himself as Son of Man and thus begins to transform his disciples' expectation of the Davidic King. In verses 31–32, Jesus begins explaining "what sort of Messiah" he will be.[65] In 8:38, the Son of Man has "his *Father's* angels" with him, and "Son of God" is a messianic title with its roots in 2 Samuel 7 and Psalm 2. This Son of Man will be the conquering leader in the end (8:38), but will suffer, be rejected, die and be raised before all of that (8:31). Collins goes so far as to say that Mark's presentation indicates "a shared assumption [between Mark and his readers] of the Davidic or royal messiah and a shared assumption that 'messiah' in this sense and 'Son of Man' are equivalent."[66] It is striking however that while statements about Jesus as Christ are not to be told, Jesus calls the crowd to listen to statements about the Son of Man.

This public character of the Son of Man and his activity makes for a sharp difference with the Son of Man spoken about in the Similitudes.[67] In contrast to a hidden figure, only revealed in the eschaton, Jesus uses Son of Man to publicly identify himself and his fate both immediately and eschatologically. Thus, while there will be a final revelation, taking some by surprise, the Markan Son of Man is not hidden in the meantime. Indeed, a person's fate in the eschaton is explicitly described as depending upon knowing, and being faithful to him, in the meantime. This is the first Son of Man statement in Mark to have clear eschatological overtones and the authority is much more like a Danielic Son of Man, in setting and style. What is mild allusion to Daniel here, however, will move more toward quotation later on in Mark's story.

Mark 9:9–13

The Scene (9:9–13)

This short scene is transitioning out of the transfiguration scene (9:2–8) and into another demoniac cleansing (9:14–29). It is differentiated from the transfiguration by the physical change in scene—Jesus and his inner circle of disciples (Peter, James, and John) are now descending from the mountain

---

65. Marcus, *Mark*, 613.

66. Collins, *Mark*, 402; a similar point is made in Collins and Collins, *King and Messiah*, 150–52.

67. Collins, *Mark*, 402–3; though it should be noted that the relationship to the messiah is a strong point of affinity; cf. Collins and Collins, *King and Messiah*, 86–94, 168.

(9:9). Since the scene is a single discussion, verses 11–12 will be discussed between the two sayings.

The scene does, however, draw significantly on what has transpired in the transfiguration itself. Whatever is made of the transfiguration regarding its historicity and original setting,[68] Mark's Gospel simply presents it as part of the story. On the mountain with just three of his disciples, Jesus's appearance is changed, and his clothes become dazzling white. He has a conversation with long-dead prophets: Moses and Elijah. When Peter, whom Mark describes as confused, suggests the building of tents for the three leaders, a cloud envelops them. From the cloud comes what must be assumed is the voice of God: Ο ὗτός ἐστιν ὁ υἱός μου ὁ ἀγαπητός, ἀκούετε αὐτοῦ. At this point the cloud clears and only Jesus is present before the disciples. The transfiguration has thus conveyed a very high Christology, emphasizing Jesus's glory, his association with Scripture and its heroes, his relationship with God as beloved son, and the demand that he be heard. This is only displayed to a few of the disciples, "but it will soon become part of their joyful proclamation to the world."[69]

The Saying (9:9)

The first of the two sayings is again in indirect speech. Jesus orders his disciples not to reveal their experience of his transfiguration, the appearance of Elijah and Moses, and the approving voice of God, εἰ μὴ ὅταν ὁ υἱὸς τοῦ ἀνθρώπου ἐκ νεκρῶν ἀναστῇ (9:9). This is the final "command to silence" in Mark's Gospel and is the only one to restrict proclamation for a set period—until after the first Easter.[70] Restricting their speaking about this glorification experience until after Jesus has risen (and thus completed the entirety of the mission described in 8:31) ensures that while these core disciples receive an encouraging glimpse of Jesus's resurrection glory they cannot think that it will somehow come without the suffering, rejection, and death.[71] Nor should they, by speaking about these things, encourage "the wrong sort of messianic enthusiasm."[72] Mark's retelling of this statement also indicates that Jesus's resurrection has indeed happened, since the information is being distributed.

68. For discussion see e.g. Marcus, *Mark*, 636–37, 1108–18; Edwards, *Gospel*, 269–71.
69. Marcus, *Mark*, 642.
70. Edwards, *Gospel*, 272.
71. Edwards, *Gospel*, 273; Collins, *Mark*, 429; Moloney, *Gospel of Mark*, 181.
72. France, *Gospel of Mark*, 356.

The Scene (9:10–11)

The disciples accept Jesus's restriction, but there is an internal debate about what the resurrection of the dead meant. Whether this debate was internal to each disciple or among the group depends somewhat on whether πρὸς ἑαυτούς is read with ἐκράτησαν or συζητοῦντες.[73] Edwards points out that it is unlikely the disciples doubted that there was a resurrection,[74] but says that their concern relates to the fact that, "If the Son of Man is to be raised, he must first die. The disciples are unprepared for any thought that the Messiah must suffer and die before his entrance into glory."[75] This may be part of their discussion, but the disciples could—to this point—have expected Jesus's resurrection and the general resurrection and eschatological judgment to occur at the same time, whereas now, Jesus has placed a proclamation time between his resurrection (8:31) and the eschatological judgment (8:38).[76] If the disciples were only at this point coming to realize that there may be a distinction in timing between Jesus's resurrection and a general resurrection, then it would no doubt precipitate much thought and consternation.

If their internal debate related in part to this issue of timing, this would also make good sense of their following question, for it concerns the nature and timing of an Elijah figure. Some recent scholarship has suggested that the expectation was that Elijah would come before the eschaton rather than specifically before the Messiah (cf. Mal 4:5—the day of Yahweh).[77] Their question is especially significant since they have just seen Elijah privately on the mountain but cannot speak about him, and if the expectation is of a public ministry from Elijah this makes their experience and the silencing that much stranger. So, rather than being only an attempt to "rebut the implication of suffering" through an appeal to the idea that Elijah would make the way smooth for the Messiah,[78] the disciples have reason to seek clarity regarding Elijah, the general eschatological resurrection and Jesus's own resurrection. Jesus's answer to their question includes the second of these two Son of Man sayings and gives some insight into their debate about what "rising from the dead" means.

---

73. Omanson and Metzger, *Textual Guide*, 82.

74. So also Marcus, *Mark*, 648.

75. Edwards, *Gospel*, 273.

76. This "specific rising" and its timing are issues also suggested in Marcus, *Mark*, 643, 648; Van Iersel, *Mark*, 298; Collins, *Mark*, 429–30; Focant, *According to Mark*, 361–62; Moloney, *Gospel of Mark*, 181; Gundry, *Mark*, 463–64, 483–84.

77. For discussion of this issue see Marcus, *Mark*, 644; Van Iersel, *Mark*, 298–99.

78. As described by Edwards, *Gospel*, 273.

The Saying (9:12–13)

Jesus first appears to affirm the expectation of an Elijah figure and his extensive restorative work.[79] Before the disciples can ask, Jesus anticipates their response with a Son of Man saying: καὶ πῶς γέγραπται ἐπὶ τὸν υἱὸν τοῦ ἀνθρώπου ἵνα πολλὰ πάθῃ καὶ ἐξουδενηθῇ; Casey suggests that here Son of Man has particular reference to John/Elijah,[80] but such a view fails to consider that in this context Jesus has just mentioned the Son of Man rising from the dead, which refers back to 8:31.[81] Rather, Jesus is posing a riddle about how Elijah can perform a restorative and preparative work and yet the Messiah subsequently suffers.[82]

In his statement about the Son of Man, as in 8:31, there is a reference to significant suffering,[83] but instead of rejection and death, the Son of Man is treated contemptuously, though ἀποδοκιμάζω and ἐξουδενέω are close in their meaning.[84] Instead of it simply "being necessary," Jesus makes explicit reference to the Son of Man's treatment being able to be found in Scripture, but he does not give more explicit reference as to which particular passages generate that expectation.[85] Thus the saying is a second "passion prediction," explicitly relating it to the Old Testament and adding nuance to the expectation already set in 8:31.

In verse 13 Jesus solves that riddle of how two, seemingly incompatible, statements can be held together: Elijah prepares the way for the Lord and the Son of Man is still be treated terribly. The solution is by no means

---

79. Marcus favors the reading in Codex Bezae that Jesus is asking a question here and so not affirming but questioning this conclusion. His reasoning works, but the textual evidence is too scant to support it. I prefer to think that Jesus is affirming yet transforming the nature of Elijah's preparative work as will be outlined below. In any case, this is not the section that really matters. Marcus, *Mark*, 644–45. And see Gundry's brief critique, Gundry, *Mark*, 484–85.

80. Though he also says it has reference to Jesus as fits his general and specific idiomatic interpretation. The problem in this case arose with the translation for non-bilingual (i.e. Greek and Aramaic) readers in subsequent generations. Casey, *Aramaic Sources*, 126–37, esp. 132, 135.

81. Focant, *According to Mark*, 362. Casey has no problem with isolating the sayings from their context, nor ruling out aspects of the canonical text which do not fit his theory. Casey, *Aramaic Sources*, 135; Casey, *Solution*, 116–21.

82. So also, Gundry, *Mark*, 484–85.

83. See above about the adverbial use of πολλά.

84. Collins, *Mark*, 431; France, *Gospel of Mark*, 360.

85. Scholars again suggest many options. Common among them are Pss 22; 69; 118:22; Isa 53; and Dan 7:13–14 when linked with verses 18, 21–22, 25–27. E.g. France, *Gospel of Mark*, 359–60; Marcus, *Mark*, 645; Van Iersel, *Mark*, 300; Collins, *Mark*, 430–31; Gundry, *Mark*, 485.

simple but is found in the idea that "Elijah" has already come and "prepared the way" by being treated terribly himself by the leaders. "It is generally agreed that the Markan Jesus refers to John the Baptist in saying, 'Elijah has indeed come,' and Matthew makes this explicit (17:3)."[86] Thus Jesus both affirms their expectation of Elijah, yet drastically transforms the nature of that expectation, and like that of the Son of Man, his treatment was as "it is written."[87] Jesus also answers the question of timing by saying that what was required regarding Elijah had already occurred.

The Emerging Picture of the Son of Man (9:9–13)

Together these two Son of Man sayings reiterate and expand the ideas of 8:31. Reiteration is seen in the latter as referring to great suffering and a scornful treatment of the Son of Man, and in the former referring to a subsequent resurrection of the Son of Man, which must also by definition expect his death. The scriptural reference(s) in mind and the specificity of the relationship with Elijah, who is generally held to be John the Baptist, remain undefined but these expand and clarify the sense in which the suffering of 8:31 was necessary. This explicit reference to something happening as γέγραπται indicates that Jesus's prediction of the Son of Man's death has its origins in Scripture. This, along with an association with the promised Elijah, not to mention the details of the transfiguration which has just taken place, could well signify that the Son of Man and especially his death, is critical to God's plans. The reference to the Son of Man's resurrection in the early saying indicates that there is a distinction in timing between the Son of Man's resurrection and a final general resurrection and judgment, since that would be the time when the disciples would be able to speak about the transfiguration scene. Any reader of Mark, who was not already aware, must also appreciate that since the transfiguration testimony is now public, the Son of Man must have already risen from the dead.

---

86. Collins, *Mark*, 432. "It is certainly [John the Baptist] who hides behind the figure of Elijah." Focant, *According to Mark*, 362.

87. What precisely "was written" concerning Elijah, and the relationship with John the Baptist, and how John can prepare for Jesus in both a positive and a negative way is beyond the scope of this study to answer. Writing of John the Baptist, Webb has the opposite problem, calling "the interjection of a reference to the Son of Man" "problematic" but he concludes "John's suffering and death as 'Elijah' paves the way for, and prefigures the similar fate of Jesus as the Son of Man." Webb, *John the Baptiser*, 53–54. Contra Taylor, *Immerser*, 281–88. See also Murphy, *John the Baptist*, 76–77, 130–31; Wink, *Gospel Tradition*, 13–17.

The theme of conflict and rejection seen in the previous sayings is again apparent here, but other themes are less apparent. The conflict/rejection idea is particularly evident in the latter saying—πολλὰ πάθη καὶ ἐξουδενηθῇ, but it is not entirely missing from verse 9, which assumes the death of Jesus. A supreme present authority, on the other hand, so dominant in the sayings of chapter 2, does not fit in this context, though Jesus does command his disciples and interpret Scripture. So too a final eschatological vindication is not brought to the fore, even though it might readily have been referred to given that the disciples ask a question about Malachi 4:5.

Mark 9:30–32

The Scene (9:30–32)

Like the previous setting, this scene is also transitional as Jesus moves privately from somewhere outside and then through Galilee (v. 30), with the next scene beginning in Capernaum (v. 33). While Galilee has been prominent thus far in Mark's geographical setting, this is the final time events will take place in Galilee until after the resurrection (14:28; 16:7).[88] The progression of Jesus and his disciples is generally southward having been in Caesarea Philippi (8:27).

The explanation for that privacy is that Jesus was teaching his disciples (v. 31a). The content of his teaching is described in the next Son of Man saying. The reason for the privacy, however, may not have been the content of the Son of Man saying per se, but the disciples' lack of understanding and fear about questioning it. That is, the explanation stretches to the end of verse 32 and involves not just the idea of Jesus's instruction but also the response from his disciples. Understood this way, the secrecy of movement allows for Jesus's private tuition of reluctant disciples about the Son of Man, while preventing them from spreading any misunderstanding in the meantime. This would thus be distinguished from the privacy and silencing previously seen in Mark's Gospel (e.g. 1:34, 44; 8:30) and cohere with the way Jesus was more explicit with his disciples (8:31) while allowing for a public and more implicit description of his demise among the crowd (8:34–38). "Jesus' mission is now to teach his disciples, and that takes priority over any public activity" (cf. 4:34; 7:17; 9:28).[89] The disciples do not understand how what Jesus says will happen, and their "reluctance ἐπερωτῆσαι, 'to ask,'

---

88. Edwards, *Gospel*, 283.
89. France, *Gospel of Mark*, 371.

Jesus for further clarification no doubt results from their fear that Jesus will underscore yet again the certainty of his death."[90]

The Saying (9:31)

The use of the imperfect tense forms, ἐδίδασκεν and ἔλεγεν, are probably intended to convey an iterative *Aktionsart*.[91] That is, this was repeated teaching through this period of travel. It is also iterative in a broader sense within Mark's narrative, that is, he returns to the same ideas a number of times (see comment above on Mark 8:31).[92] What follows then, is likely only a summary of a larger discourse on the matter. Yet in spite of Jesus making space for them, Mark reports that the disciples neither had clarity about this matter, nor did they actively seek it (v. 32).[93]

This core information is very similar to the trajectory set out for the Son of Man in Mark 8:31. There are, however, a few important differences, namely in the phrase παραδίδοται εἰς χεῖρας ἀνθρώπων. The use of the present tense form here could indicate that the events have already started to happen.[94] That is, the imperfective aspect and spatial proximity of the present tense form in this context might convey progressive *Aktionsart*. However, since παραδίδωμι is a verb of "propulsion" the use of an imperfective tense form may be associated with this kind of lexeme, and thus it can be credibly interpreted as a "future occurrence" using the present tense form.[95] In either case, however, the completion of the handing over lies in the future.

---

90. Evans, *Mark 8:27—16:20*, 58; so also Moloney, *Gospel of Mark*, 187–88; Focant, *According to Mark*, 376. Strauss suggests that the "simplest solution" for their reluctance relates to Jesus having accused them of "spiritual dullness" (4:13; 7:18; 8:18, 21). Strauss, *Mark*, 408. Now, certainly their spiritual dullness is confirmed by their lack of understanding and reluctance, and perhaps there is a sense in which they did not wish to admit this, but given the privacy that Jesus has given them they need not "fear" public shaming.

91. Campbell, *Indicative Mood*, 77–102; Campbell, *Basics of Verbal Aspect*, 77–78.

92. France, *Gospel of Mark*, 371.

93. Marcus notes this as the correct reading of the text, yet says that it points to a reconstruction by Mark. This however need not be the case, as it is surely not too surprising that a group of students refused to be engaged and properly comprehend something they did not want to hear. Marcus, *Mark*, 668–69.

94. France, *Gospel of Mark*, 371.

95. Though their understanding of the aspect of Greek verbs might be different both to mine and to each other, these authors agree on the idea of a "future referring" present being read here. Marcus, *Mark*, 667; Collins, *Mark*, 440. Marcus cites Fanning, *Verbal Aspect*, 225. See also Campbell, *Indicative Mood*, 35–76, esp. 52.

What is less clear is who is responsible for this passive idea.[96] It could be God handing him over, which would make it agree with the sense of necessity and scriptural warrant already seen (8:31, 9:12).[97] In particular, the verbal link with Isaiah 53:6 in the LXX is striking—κύριος παρέδωκεν αὐτὸν ταῖς ἁμαρτίαις ἡμῶν.[98] More likely, however, this is hinting at a betrayal, since this would agree with Mark's introduction of Judas (3:19) and with the events later in the story.[99] Perhaps the ambiguity reflects that of 14:21 which recognizes both divine and human agencies behind the actions, though it only uses παραδίδωμι in relation to the human. In fact, παραδίδωμι is almost invariably used in Mark's Gospel negatively of human actors.[100] Finally, the use of ἀνθρώπων broadens the sense of rejection and execution of the Son of Man from Jewish leaders to all humanity.[101] These men are responsible for killing him. Yet, as he has before, Jesus points to a resurrection μετὰ τρεῖς ἡμέρας.

The Emerging Picture of the Son of Man (9:30–32)

This very brief episode offers the third reiteration of the imminent fate of the Son of Man: he will be killed and rise again. It is both an example of the repetition expected from 8:31 (see comments above) and implies that Jesus spoke about it over a period of time with his disciples. That Jesus spent this time alone with his disciples attempting to have them understand what is going to happen to him shows both his certainty of the imminent fate of the Son of Man, and his desire for the disciples to understand it (as well as perhaps the surprising/difficult nature of the content of this material for the disciples).

Beyond simple repetition, the scene progresses the theme of conflict and rejection in two ways. Firstly, and most significantly, the saying introduces a possibility of betrayal with the word παραδίδωμι. Though it might be read as a divine passive, given the information of 3:19, and Mark's wider

---

96. For a view similar to that which is presented here see Collins, *Mark*, 440–41.

97. Those who hold the "divine passive" view include: Stein, *Mark*, 439; Hooker, *Commentary*, 226; Witherington, *Gospel of Mark*, 268–69; Edwards, *Gospel*, 284; Moloney, *Gospel of Mark*, 187; Focant, *According to Mark*, 376.

98. Culpepper, *Mark*, 309.

99. Gundry is even stronger in stating this view. Gundry, *Mark*, 506–7.

100. The exceptions to this are 10:33, where it is used the same way as it is here, and 7:13 where Jesus speaks of the tradition "handed down," though perhaps there Jesus is subtly accusing them of betraying their own tradition.

101. Edwards, *Gospel*, 283; Stein, *Mark*, 439–40.

story, it would not be hard to see this as the first insinuation by Jesus of Judas's betrayal. If it is a divine passive then the use of the present tense form may point to the idea that this is already in progress, though it is more likely that a future-referring present tense form should be read, and, in any case, completion will not come for some time. This fills out the picture as to how the Son of Man will be able to be condemned by the leaders of the people—how he will be "in their hands." Secondly, as there was in 8:32, there is also a sense of discord between Jesus and his disciples through this Son of Man scene. Though he has afforded them time and space away from the crowds to teach them, they do not understand, and do not seek clarification, and this in spite of the fact that he is their rabbi and the one whom they have identified as the Christ. In sum, Son of Man is once again linked to rejection and conflict and after his "handing over" he will face death and then rise again.

Mark 10:32–45

The Scene (10:32–45)

While it is not unusual for commentators to divide Jesus's passion prediction in verses 32–34 from the discussion precipitated by James and John's request in verses 35–45, in this analysis they belong to the same scene and will be dealt with together.[102] They are both part of the discussion "on the way to Jerusalem" (v. 32) and the geographical setting only changes when they reach Jericho (v. 46). In fact, Mark uses καί at verse 35 which marks continuity rather than leaving the clause unmarked or specifically marking a development with another conjunction.[103]

There is however a striking contrast in the attitude of the disciples between the two subsections. In the former they are astonished and afraid, apparently lagging behind Jesus (v. 32),[104] while in the latter James and John are bold enough to ask Jesus for prominent positions and express a willingness to endure what Jesus will endure. The others are indignant about this request (vv. 35, 37, 39, 41). This contrast is somewhat lessened if οἱ ἀκολουθοῦντες is a broader group than the twelve (v. 32)—thus making

---

102. So also Moloney, *Gospel of Mark*, 203–8; Van Iersel, *Mark*, 331–38; Witherington, *Gospel of Mark*, 285–93 (though, he extends the episode to v. 52); Strauss, *Mark*, 452–64; France, *Gospel of Mark*, 409–21.

103. Runge, *Discourse Grammar*, 23–27.

104. Edwards, *Gospel*, 318; Moloney, *Gospel of Mark*, 204.

the twelve more astonished (θαμβέω) than specifically afraid (φοβέω).¹⁰⁵ In any case, this sort of ambivalence is not uncommon in Mark's story,¹⁰⁶ and the disciples have had discussions about greatness in the preceding chapter in which John is prominent (9:33–41). To both their fear and their boldness, Jesus responds with private words to the disciples about the Son of Man (vv. 32, 42).

The Saying (10:32b–34)

In introducing this saying, the narrator underscores that Jesus was talking about himself as Son of Man—these are τὰ μέλλοντα αὐτῷ συμβαίνειν. Jesus also uses the first person plural, ἀναβαίνομεν, which points to a personal involvement as well as having ominous implications for the disciples.¹⁰⁷ Aside from drawing attention to what is to come,¹⁰⁸ the use of ἰδού likely brings this saying into line with the genre of prophetic oracle. As Evans notes, "He does not tell the disciples what he suspects might happen; he tells them what will in fact happen. The use of συμβαίνειν in the sense of what 'happens' is common in the LXX (e.g., Gen 41:13; 42:4, 29; 44:29; Exod 1:10; 3:16; Job 1:22; Esth 6:13; 1 Macc 4:26)."¹⁰⁹ Mark wants his readers to be sure that Jesus "knew the precise details of what would be involved, but he nevertheless went because this was a divine necessity."¹¹⁰

As in 9:31, Jesus's first verb is a present indicative—ἀναβαίνομεν—and here there can be no question that the chain of events described has already begun. Unlike 9:31, the παραδίδωμι is given in the future tense form, which is restricted to being future with respect to the setting.¹¹¹ Thus all the subsequent events happen after they reach Jerusalem (especially since that is where the chief priests are). In this instance there are also two "handing over" events. The first is passive as the Son of Man is given τοῖς ἀρχιερεῦσιν καὶ τοῖς γραμματεῦσιν. It is possible that this is a divine passive (as with 9:31

---

105. Cf. the discussion of these questions in Culpepper, *Mark*, 342–43; Stein, *Mark*, 479; Marcus, *Mark*, 741–42.

106. E.g. Peter's response to Jesus 8:29, 32; 14:29, 66–72.

107. Edwards, *Gospel*, 318. In fact, Jesus will describe the need for James and John to suffer similar fates as him in vv. 38–39, and this may account for why Mark maintains the proximity of these two juxtaposed stories.

108. Gundry, *Mark*, 572.

109. Evans, *Mark 8:27—16:20*, 108.

110. Stein, *Mark*, 480.

111. Unlike other tense forms, the future is semantically constrained to present future events. Campbell, *Indicative Mood*, 159–60.

ambiguity remains), though given the human involvement in the second use of παραδίδωμι, the idea of betrayal by a human agent would be likely.[112] After the group condemns him to death, they give him (active voice) to the gentiles who are responsible for the events that follow. This prediction goes on to add more detail of the Son of Man's suffering previously presented in Mark's story, in that the gentiles will mock, spit on, and flog him, before they kill him.[113]

Historical questions have not been a major focus in this analysis, but the distinction between Jesus's prediction here and Mark's description in 15:15, where φραγελλοῦν is used instead of μαστιγώσουσιν, should be understood as an example of multiple attestation. It encourages understanding of this prediction as historical in nature.[114] As Evans notes, "This lack of agreement between prediction and subsequent narrative *favors* the independence, if not authenticity, of the prediction."[115]

For the third time the predicted death is followed by resurrection (μετὰ τρεῖς ἡμέρας). The textual variation on this prediction is best accounted for by copyists bringing the text into line with parallels in Matt 20:19 and Luke 18:33 and other resurrection texts which use the temporal dative τῇ τρίτῃ ἡμέρᾳ.[116]

The Saying (10:42–45)

Jesus's second word to the twelve in this scene is designed to answer the questions of authority and power among the disciples. In verse 42, Jesus points to the normal pattern of behavior in the world with regard to those "considered as rulers of the gentiles" (οἱ δοκοῦντες ἄρχειν τῶν ἐθνῶν); how they flaunt any power and exploit their subjects. Then, in verse 43a, he excludes such behavior from among his disciples before giving the positive command in verses 43b–44 about how they should serve. It is an inversion of the normal pattern in that greatness is determined by servanthood and

---

112. Marcus's discussion is comprehensive as he considers the language of the Servant Songs of Isaiah but also the relationship to Judas elsewhere in the Gospel (3:19; 14:10, 18 etc.) and concludes that there is an "intersection of the divine and human wills" in a similar way to that described in 14:18 and 14:21. Marcus, *Mark*, 742, 745–46.

113. So also Focant, *According to Mark*, 422.

114. Contra Moloney, *Gospel of Mark*, 204.

115. Evans, *Mark 8:27—16:20*, 109, emphasis mine; cf. Focant, *According to Mark*, 424; Stein, *Mark*, 477–78. Focant claims disagreement with Evans, but overstates what Evans concludes, so they may actually be in general agreement, hence my use of emphasis.

116. Omanson and Metzger, *Textual Guide*, 89.

preeminence by slavery. This pattern of behavior is explained (γάρ) by the similar (καί should be again be understood as ascensive or adverbially comparative here) behavior of the Son of Man: ὁ υἱὸς τοῦ ἀνθρώπου οὐκ ἦλθεν διακονηθῆναι ἀλλὰ διακονῆσαι. This is significant in that it underscores that the disciples are not being asked to do anything different to their master: voluntary self-effacing service.

The final clause of the saying demonstrates that the preeminent act of service by the Son of Man is in making a transactional and sacrificial offering of his life. Jesus must be speaking about his death—δοῦναι τὴν ψυχὴν— and in context he predicted his death and resurrection (10:31–32) and has just been solemnly speaking about his "baptism" and "cup" in clear relation to his death. The language of δίδωμι is cultic, especially when used in conjunction with service and death. λύτρον ἀντὶ πολλῶν evokes a slave market; it is the price of release for many. Marcus suggests, "The servitude imagery of the previous verses and the use of *diakonein* in the present context favor the view that this ransom is conceived as a slave price: Jesus sells himself into slavery in order to liberate his brothers and sisters from bondage."[117] Moreover, the language of ἦλθεν is missional and thus related to the ἀναβαίνοντες of verse 32. Jesus's language here may have a background in the Servant Songs of Isaiah and particularly 53:10–12.[118] The themes of service, giving life in sacrifice, and acting for many in doing so, have clear parallels in these texts. The language of ransom is not found directly in the Servant Songs, but instead the language is that "he bore the sin of many and made intercession for the transgressors" (53:12).[119] Interpreted as background, this would provide some clarity regarding the nature of the transaction Jesus makes in his death.[120] Moreover, ransom language is not far from the Servant Songs, being found in Isaiah 43:3–4.[121] While not directly quoting or translating Isaiah, Jesus could well be understood as offering "a summary of the task of the Servant,"[122] and saying that he, the Son of Man, fulfills the servant's mission through his death. Whatever can be made of this significant background, France aptly points out that "Jesus is not just quoting the OT. He

---

117. Marcus, *Mark*, 757.

118. Edwards, *Gospel*, 327–28; Evans, *Mark 8:27—16:20*, 120–24; France, *Gospel of Mark*, 419–21; Marcus, *Mark*, 750, 756–57; Stein, *Mark*, 488–89; Culpepper, *Mark*, 349–50.

119. Cf. Culpepper, *Mark*, 350.

120. Evans, *Mark 8:27—16:20*, 121.

121. Evans, *Mark 8:27—16:20*, 122–23; Following Grimm, *Weil Ich Dich Liebe*, 231–77; Stuhlmacher, "Vicariously Giving," 22–26.

122. Evans, *Mark 8:27—16:20*, 121.

is making a statement about his own mission."[123] The Son of Man's death has been predicted multiple times, spoken of as necessary and according to God's plan laid out in Scripture, and now a definitive outcome is tied to it: it is a sacrifice and release payment for many in the style of Isaiah's suffering servant.

The Emerging Picture of the Son of Man (10:32–45)

Thus, Mark's narrative has three consistent predictions by Jesus of the Son of Man's fate: the Son of Man (by which Jesus refers to himself) will suffer, die, and rise again μετὰ τρεῖς ἡμέρας. This final prediction confirms elements already seen in one or other of the previous predictions: an idea of handing over and the condemnation by Sanhedrin members. As has been seen all along, this saying links rejection by Jewish authorities with the Son of Man. It also adds key information: the location of Jerusalem, the role of gentiles in carrying out the condemnation of Jewish leaders, and the specifics of the suffering which the Son of Man will endure. Jesus "strides on ahead toward his destiny in Jerusalem,"[124] and the Gospel prepares "the listening audience for the passion narrative that follows, building suspense but also focusing their attention and alerting them as to what to expect."[125] The disciples also have their shock and any fear of Jesus's future addressed through the prediction of death and resurrection. The scourge and crucifixion will not be a tragedy, but will fulfill God's plan according to prophecy,[126] and the passive endurance of the Son of Man will be followed by his active rising.[127]

Jesus previously spoke of the Son of Man's death as necessary and in line with the expectation of "what is written," but for the first time, Jesus offers direct interpretation of the death of the Son of Man. In this episode, Jesus, likely drawing on Isaianic themes, speaks of his mission as the Son of Man to go to Jerusalem and offer his life sacrificially, slaving for his disciples, bringing the release of many.

As the first saying addresses more directly the disciples' negative expectations, the second addresses their positive ones—those of power and comfort. Jesus just said that at least two of his disciples will "share in this victory by being 'baptized' into the messianic suffering that brings it to pass,"[128]

123. France, *Gospel of Mark*, 421.
124. Moloney, *Gospel of Mark*, 204.
125. Collins, *Mark*, 486.
126. So also Stein, *Mark*, 481.
127. Marcus, *Mark*, 745.
128. Marcus, *Mark*, 746.

and then all of the disciples are called to be like the Son of Man and seek to serve, if they would lead.[129] Thus the Son of Man's authority is raised, but unlike the authority seen in chapter 2, it is clearly an inverted authority. Thus, the Son of Man uses his immense authority to serve self-sacrificially.

Mark 13:24–37

The Scene (13:24–37)

In accordance with the method established, the scene for this Son of Man saying begins at 13:3 with a private question from the disciples on the Mount of Olives. The scene concludes with Jesus's command to be alert (13:37) and a new time and characters are introduced in 14:1. Broadly speaking, Mark 13 concludes a series of episodes set in or about the temple from Mark 11 and offers Jesus's explanation for his prophecy of the temple's destruction (13:1–2). Given the length of this discourse and the contention associated with it, it is too bold to attempt to view the scene in detail. Instead, attention will be focused on the scene within a scene, since there are clear markers of distinction made at verse 24 and then in verse 28.

In verse 23, Jesus had been instructing his disciples to be aware of what he has predicted for them, but in verse 24 he moves to a time (μετὰ τὴν θλῖψιν ἐκείνην) and speaks not of them seeing but of unnamed subjects seeing (ὄψονται), and the use of ἀλλά marks what follows as a kind of correction to the preceding material.[130] The sense of "correction" that verses 24–27 offer with regard to the preceding material is thus not difficult to understand: Jesus began his answer to the disciples' question with a warning about deception regarding his personal arrival (vv. 5–6) and in verses 21–23 Jesus warns of false reports about the presence of the Christ during the tribulation, intended to mislead the elect. Now Jesus speaks of something after that tribulation which is the cataclysmically unmissable coming of the Son of Man. In verse 28, another development marker is used (δὲ) and Jesus returns to second person imperatives. There are also changes in time and imagery. The scene within the discourse is set ἐν ἐκείναις ταῖς ἡμέραις, a common—yet not exclusive[131]—introduction for eschatological

---

129. Interestingly the themes of sacrifice and leadership are also found just after the Son of Man saying in 9:31 (though it comes in a distinct scene after the geographical change at 9:33). To a lesser extent 8:31—9:1 picks up these themes too (where there is an invitation to walk and die with the Son of Man, a concept of promised glory but not a specific discussion of greatness).

130. For ἀλλά as marking correction see Runge, *Discourse Grammar*, 55–56.

131. It can be used in more mundane contexts as throughout the book of Judges. Gundry, *Mark*, 782.

prophecy in the Old Testament (e.g. Jer 3:16; Joel 2:28; Zech 8:23), and at a time beyond the θλῖψις of verse 19. It involves events of cosmic upheaval common to apocalypses: the sun, moon, and stars do the opposite to what they usually do, while certain heavenly δυνάμεις are shaken. Focant aptly shows that this description draws heavily on the LXX of Isaiah (cf. 13:10; 34:4 incl. var.).[132] These drastic changes allow for a new world order and the final apocalyptic theophany—the coming, not of God per se, but of the Son of Man.[133] Though her reasoning differs at points to that presented here, Collins concludes correctly that, "vv. 24-27 should be taken not only as a separate literary unit but also as the portrayal of the final stage in the eschatological drama."[134]

The Saying (13:26–27)

The Son of Man "coming in the clouds" would always convey overtones of majesty since it indicates authority over the forces of nature. When seen against the background of the Danielic vision (7:13–14), where one "like a son of man" comes on the clouds to be eternally given all authority by God himself, those overtones are to be understood in the superlative. Though clearly dependent on Daniel, the Greek used is not bound to the LXX (or another Greek version). Jesus speaks of the Son of Man ἐν νεφέλαις not ἐπὶ τῶν νεφελῶν and uses δύναμις rather than ἐξουσία.[135] This variance would need to be explained by anyone who sees this as an early emendation or addition by a scribe familiar with the LXX phrasing.[136] Power and glory are spoken of in the Old Testament as belonging to God or as that which God has distributed to mighty kings (e.g. Ps 62:3; 1 Chr 29:11; Dan 2:3; 4:30).[137] The "great power" with which the Son of Man comes is most likely the angelic army whom he sends in verse 27.[138] Thus the Son of Man would

---

132. Focant, *According to Mark*, 546.

133. Given the changes of time and imagery I do not think that this view suffers from a "generation problem" as suggested by Bolt, but there is not space in this book to map out the timing and interpretation of the other aspects of Jesus's discussion in chapter 13, and their precise relationship to the passion narrative that follows. Cf. Peter Bolt, *Cross from a Distance*, esp. 94–96.

134. Collins, *Mark*, 614.

135. Focant, *According to Mark*, 546–47.

136. As Gundry observes, "None of these counter arguments prove authenticity or disprove Marcan or earlier redaction, but they do expose weaknesses in the denial of the dominical tradition." Gundry, *Mark*, 784.

137. Evans, *Mark 8:27—16:20*, 329.

138. Gundry, *Mark*, 768.

readily be understood as a supreme agent of the Almighty God, if not divine in his own right.

Those who witness the arrival of the Son of Man "remain indefinite."[139] The most direct subject grammatically would have to be the celestial bodies and heavenly powers of verses 24-25.[140] Alternatively, Jesus's later response in 14:62 points toward members of the Sanhedrin and other leaders,[141] as well the early reference to such authorities in conflict with the disciples (v. 9). Other options would have to include the false Christs of verse 22, the elect of verse 27, or a combination of these groups or even all people. Though specifying this group would add some nuance to the scene presented, the main point is that there will certainly be an appearance of the Son of Man in ultimate supremacy.

Rather than executing condemnation, as might be expected after such an apocalyptic introduction, the Son of Man then directs angels to gather in his chosen ones—τοὺς ἐκλεκτοὺς αὐτοῦ (13:27).[142] Given what they have just been told to expect—severe persecution (vv. 9-13) and other turmoil (vv. 7-8, 14-20)—this gathering is a salvific act for disciples of Jesus. Though not made explicit, there is an expectation of blessing to follow their patient endurance for Jesus's sake (cf. v. 13). The area to which the angels are sent covers not just the physical earth (the four winds, cf. Zech 2:10) but the entirety of the cosmos—ἀπ' ἄκρου γῆς ἕως ἄκρου οὐρανοῦ.[143] Regardless of where the elect are in life or death, these angels will find them.

The Emerging Picture of the Son of Man (13:24-37)

This saying affirms the contours of the authority of the Son of Man already seen in Mark's Gospel even as it moves beyond them. His authority (vv. 26-27; cf. 2:1-12, 23-28), association with messianic expectation (vv. 21-23, cf. 2:23-28; 8:29-31), having "glory" and commanding "angels" (8:38) are reiterated, but now the Son of Man is presented as "the subject of the theophany."[144] He appears at the end of the age of normal things, the cul-

---

139. Focant, *According to Mark*, 544.
140. See discussion in Marcus, *Mark*, 903-4.
141. So Gundry, *Mark*, 783; Evans, *Mark 8:27—16:20*, 329.
142. So Focant, *According to Mark*, 544; Stein, *Mark*, 615; Collins, *Mark*, 614-15. Note the text variance here—which omits αὐτοῦ after angels and elect—is not significant enough to warrant discussion in Omanson's *Textual Guide*, but there is a paragraph found in Marcus, *Mark*, 905.
143. So also Gundry, *Mark*, 786.
144. Stein, *Mark*, 616.

mination of the cosmic upheaval, in the position of God over all. That Jesus once again speaks of himself as Son of Man is made clear by the sense in which the saying responds to his warnings regarding false Christs in verses 5–6 and 21–23. Pictured clearly as the Danielic Son of Man, he is given the power of God himself and uses this power to save his people.

This offers two counterpoints to themes already seen in Son of Man sayings, both of which offer clear reasons for the disciples to endure the tribulation that Jesus expects them to face. Firstly, it offers the alternative to the warning in 8:38. There the Son of Man comes and condemns those who are ashamed, and now he rescues those who remain faithful. Secondly, it responds to the clear expectation that disciples will be "with the Son of Man in suffering (8:31–38; 10:32–40; 13:9–13)."[145] The expectation is that having endured, they will have a share in his glory and power. "The Son of Man will come to gather or rescue some from all parts of the earth, but to judge and condemn others . . . no one and no place will be overlooked in the search for the saved."[146] The disciples can thus persevere through persecution and other tribulation (vv. 7–20) without fear that they will be lost or miss his arrival (vv. 6, 21–23), for in the end the Son of Man will come openly and gloriously with the armies of heaven to gather them all.[147] The Son of Man's own vindication is already to be expected in his resurrection and the shaming of those who abandon him (e.g. 8:31, 38), but for the first time, Mark's Son of Man becomes explicitly an object of eschatological hope for the disciples.

Though less directly than previously, this saying still invokes the theme of conflict and rejection of the Son of Man—the elect need rescue by the Son of Man because of their suffering for his sake at the hands of Jewish religious leaders and civic authorities (vv. 9, 13). The gathering itself also undermines the attempts of the false Christs and prophets to lead the elect astray (13:22).[148] The nuance of the conflict may be altered by who the subject of ὄψονται is interpreted to be, but this saying once again comes in a context where there is clear contrast between Jesus and his followers on the one hand, and alternative (Jewish) leaders, false believers, and teachers on the other.

---

145. Marcus, *Mark*, 909.
146. Witherington, *Gospel of Mark*, 348.
147. Hooker, *Commentary*, 319; Evans, *Mark 8:27—16:20*, 330; Stein, *Mark*, 616.
148. Marcus, *Mark*, 909.

Mark 14:17–25

The Scene (14:17–25)

This scene is set in the upper room which was, in the previous scene (vv. 12–16), prepared for Jesus and his disciples to eat the Passover. This is a private and intimate meal on one of the most important nights for faithful Jews, yet features that would make this meal a standard Passover are hardly mentioned. Instead, Mark's narrative focuses on two discourses initiated by Jesus while they are eating (ἀνακειμένων αὐτῶν καὶ ἐσθιόντων, v. 18; ἐσθιόντων αὐτῶν, v. 22). The first is Jesus's prediction of his betrayal by one of the disciples (vv. 18–21). Though the reader has clear insight into the identity of Jesus's betrayer (e.g. 3:19, 14:10–11), the disciples have only heard about the broad idea of "handing over" (9:31; 10:33), so their becoming distressed (ἤρξαντο λυπεῖσθαι) is to be expected. The Son of Man saying comes in response to the disciples' person-by-person request for exoneration—μήτι ἐγώ.[149] The second is Jesus's distribution of bread and wine to his disciples with the announcements that they are his "body" and his "blood of the covenant poured out for many" respectively (vv. 22–25). The scene ends with the singing of a hymn and their exit to the Mount of Olives (v. 26).

The Saying (14:20–21)

In spite of the fact that Jesus has just correctly predicted all the events of the meal (v. 16), the saying begins with Jesus repeating the prophecy he has just made about his betrayal (v. 17), but he adds specificity and depth to the betrayal. "'One of you' (εἷς ἐξ ὑμῶν) is restated more pointedly as 'one of the twelve' (εἷς τῶν δώδεκα)," and the broad ὁ ἐσθίων μετ' ἐμοῦ is replaced with ὁ ἐμβαπτόμενος μετ' ἐμοῦ εἰς τὸ τρύβλιον which "expresses the intimacy of the meal fellowship in a heightened way."[150] This handing over is "unnatural treachery,"[151] "a grave evil,"[152] and "heinous ... few actions were more despicable than betraying a friend at or shortly after a meal."[153]

What follows is a "μέν ... δέ" point-counterpoint construction concerning, firstly, the Son of Man and then, secondly, the betrayer of the Son

---

149. Calling it a request for an exoneration comes from Witherington, *Gospel of Mark*, 373.
150. Collins, *Mark*, 651.
151. France, *Gospel of Mark*, 556.
152. Edwards, *Gospel*, 424.
153. Brooks, *Mark*, 227.

of Man.[154] It is bound to this clause by the subordinating conjunction ὅτι and there can thus be little doubt that Jesus is speaking of himself as the Son of Man. While some consider the ὅτι to connect this verse "loosely" or "awkwardly" to the verse before,[155] and others suggest it is giving "a sense of insistence" to the idea,[156] its meaning should be considered causal, indicating a scriptural expectation that Jesus, the Son of Man, will be betrayed.[157] Why is Jesus to be betrayed? Because on the one hand (μέν) the Son of Man ὑπάγει καθὼς γέγραπται περὶ αὐτοῦ.

On the other hand (δέ),[158] the one who betrays the Son of Man is by no means excused. Rather Jesus pronounces woe τῷ ἀνθρώπῳ ἐκείνῳ. More than simply a lament,[159] this is likely a statement of condemnation,[160] since Jesus continues by saying it would be better to have never existed (than to commit such a foul act). Marcus suggests that use of the preposition διά—"'through' rather than 'by'"—is significant theologically for it preserves the sovereignty of God in being ultimately responsible for Jesus's death,[161] "despite this fatedness, however, Judas remains personally culpable."[162]

The use of ὑπάγει must eventually entail the death of the Son of Man.[163] This is not only a very old and common metaphor for death,[164] it fits entirely the context where Jesus has predicted the Son of Man being "handed over," leading to his death in accordance with God's plans as revealed in Scripture. In terms of the scriptural references Jesus has in mind, Psalm 41:9 offers the clearest allusion to the idea of betrayal after sharing friendship and a meal. Witherington also suggests Psalm 23:5 fits "just as well."[165] Such a link with Davidic Psalms would, as was also seen in Mark 2:23–28 and 8:27—9:1, build on an agreed Davidic–Jesus–Son-of-Man link among Mark and his

---

154. On point-counterpoint form and function see Runge, *Discourse Grammar*, 73–83.

155. Collins, *Mark*, 651, following others.

156. Focant, *According to Mark*, 579, following Kilpatrick.

157. So e.g. Gundry, *Mark*, 828; Evans, *Mark 8:27—16:20*, 377.

158. For the use of μέν and δέ in point-counterpoint sets see Runge, *Discourse Grammar*, 73–83.

159. Contra Focant, *According to Mark*, 575, 580.

160. Brooks, *Mark*, 228.

161. Marcus, *Mark*, 952.

162. Marcus, *Mark*, 955.

163. Contra Gundry, *Mark*, 838, who limits it to "goes to those to whom that woeful man gives over the Son of Man."

164. Marcus, *Mark*, 951.

165. Witherington, *Gospel of Mark*, 372.

audience.¹⁶⁶ This close association would not however, mean that other passages and ideas could not inform the background since Jesus's previous predictions and reference to Scripture and the divine plan have had little clear reference to any particular part of the Old Testament (8:31, 9:12–13). Evans points to Zechariah 13:7 which is quoted in 14:27, Isaiah 53, and Daniel 7 (esp. 21, 25) and 9:26 as a possible background while noting that the ambiguity of the reference makes it less likely to be a later creation.¹⁶⁷

The Emerging Picture of the Son of Man (14:17–25)

This Son of Man saying offers clarity about the nature of the way in which the Son of Man will be handed over (παραδίδωμι) to the chief priests (10:33). The Son of Man, who is none other than Jesus, is to be betrayed by a close disciple. While the readership is well prepared for it, and knows the identity of the betrayer, Mark uses this sacred Passover meal and the reaction of the rest of the disciples to highlight for his readers the utter incongruence of the action. Unsurprisingly, the betrayal of one so important (in terms of authority, fulfillment of the divine will and eschatological judgment) will not go unpunished. The Son of Man is so important that this betrayal is unforgiveable, so Judas would have been better off to have never been born rather than commit such treason. Yet the reason for this betrayal is according to God's plan and foreknowledge. "If the Son of Man must be handed over and die, it is as it is written, that is to say in conformity with the divine plan.... But the act of handing over doesn't happen any less through a human being. And it does not prevent the burden of divine judgement to weigh on the person who collaborates in the plot against Jesus."¹⁶⁸

Given this theme of betrayal there can be little doubt that this passage offers fodder to the theme of the rejection of the Son of Man already seen throughout this study. Collins's reflection on this passage captures some of the ideas which will be discussed more fully in the following chapter.

> In the context of Mark as a whole, this passage [14:17–21] continues two themes. One is the portrayal of the rejection of Jesus. The development of this theme begins with the remark about Jesus' family thinking that he was out of his mind. It continues with the offense taken and unbelief expressed by people in Jesus' hometown. It becomes explicit in Jesus' statement to Peter, James, and John that the Son of Man "is to suffer much and be

---

166. See comments above on Mark 2:23–28 and Collins, *Mark*, 652.
167. Evans, *Mark 8:27—16:20*, 377.
168. Focant, *According to Mark*, 575.

treated with contempt" in 9:12b. This saying is connected with the three passion predictions and explicitly refers to the rejection of the Son of Man as "written" (γέγραπται) concerning him. The theme also appears in the nimshal (the application) of the parable about the vine-yard and the tenants, "have you not read this scripture, 'The stone that the builders rejected has become the cornerstone. . . .'"

The other theme is that of Judas as the one who hands Jesus over to those who wish to put him to death.[169]

Finally, though beyond the Son of Man saying itself, the placement of this saying next to Jesus offering an interpretation of his death in the Last Supper is significant in that there is something similar to what was seen in 10:32–45. There Jesus predicted the Son of Man's betrayal and death and then spoke of it as a ransom for many. Here he speaks of the Son of Man's betrayal and then immediately gives his disciples his "body" and offers them "blood of the covenant poured out for many." Though the Last Supper itself is a subject of considerable scholarly discussion, (whatever else it does) it points to the sacrificial efficacy of his, the Son of Man's, death.

Mark 14:32–52

The Scene (14:32–52)

This scene takes place later on that same Passover night in Gethsemane (v. 32). It begins with Jesus asking his disciples to sit while he prays, and concludes with his arrest and the fleeing of the disciples. Emotionally, Jesus in this scene is distressed and troubled (ἐκθαμβέω, ἀδημονέω). He even says to his disciples, Περίλυπός ἐστιν ἡ ψυχή μου ἕως θανάτου. It is unsurprising that feeling like this and having been clear about his expectation would lead him to be frustrated with his disciples when he returns from his third time of prayer to find his chosen three disciples, for the third time, asleep. His response to them contains the Son of Man language and it is immediately (εὐθύς) followed by the arrival of Judas παρὰ τῶν ἀρχιερέων καὶ τῶν γραμματέων καὶ τῶν πρεσβυτέρων.

---

169. Collins, *Mark*, 648–49.

The Saying (14:41–42)

The opening three clauses καθεύδετε τὸ λοιπὸν καὶ ἀναπαύεσθε ἀπέχει are perplexing for a number of reasons. Firstly, it is not clear whether these are statements, commands, or questions. While interpreting a command would require it to be particularly sarcastic (given the command in 42a to arise),[170] each of the three options can easily convey the sense of exasperation on Jesus's part which the context demands. Secondly, τὸ λοιπόν is most commonly translated with "still" in this instance, because the more general meaning of "from now on" is not immediately intelligible. Marcus helpfully suggests that "the remainder [of the night]" is what is on view.[171] Thirdly, the function of ἀπέχει is not obvious. The word most likely conveys something being finalized (as when it is used for settled accounts), or (more commonly in the LXX) for things which are "far off" or "far away." If the former, ἀπέχει could be a statement that the disciples have had enough sleep, or it could be read with what follows and say, effectively, "the time is done."[172] Additionally, if it stands alone, this might be a further cry of exasperation: "What's the use!"[173] Or it might refer to Judas having received his payment: "He is paid."[174] Alternatively, following it as a reference to something "being far off" it could be read as a question (or perhaps even another sarcastic statement) such that Jesus's point is: "Are the disciples still sleeping? Do they think they have plenty of time since the danger, the temptation of which Jesus has spoken, is far removed?"[175] Whatever the case, these opening remarks present a frustrated Jesus offering critique of his disciples when they have been literally caught napping not only in contradiction to Jesus's repeated request, but in the moment of his greatest distress when the time he has warned of has finally come (ἦλθεν ἡ ὥρα).

Jesus had previously warned of a handing over (most recently just a few hours before 14:18–21, but also 10:33; 9:31). That he means this by speaking of ἡ ὥρα is made clear since he says ἰδοὺ παραδίδοται ὁ υἱὸς τοῦ ἀνθρώπου, then, ἰδοὺ ὁ παραδιδούς με ἤγγικεν and then Judas arrives with a crowd from the group mentioned in 8:31 and 10:33. Since Jesus interchanges Son of

---

170. Collins, *Mark*, 682.

171. Marcus, *Mark*, 980; see also the discussion in Focant, *According to Mark*, 594; Stein, *Mark*, 664; France, *Gospel of Mark*, 588.

172. France, *Gospel of Mark*, 589.

173. Edwards, *Gospel*, 436.

174. Stein, *Mark*, 664–65.

175. Evans, *Mark 8:27—16:20*, 417; reaching a similar conclusion is Marcus, *Mark*, 980–81.

Man with the first person singular pronoun, he must be speaking of himself. Furthermore, as France notes:

> παραδίδοται in verse 21 could on its own be understood either as a "divine passive" (God as the one "handing over") or quite impersonally (the Son of Man is to fall into the hands of sinners, without any indication of the agency involved). But the repetition of the verb in verse 42 with specific reference to Judas makes it clear that Jesus is speaking of the act of betrayal which he has so recently predicted (vv. 18–21).[176]

From the context, both immediately in regard to Jesus's mood, and wider within the Markan narrative, there can be no doubt that this must be an ominous moment. For his part Jesus makes this abundantly clear by describing that he is being handed εἰς τὰς χεῖρας τῶν ἁμαρτωλῶν. According to the use of the Hebraic idiom this is a condemnation (e.g. Josh 2:24; Jer 21:10; Ezek 7:21; 11:9) as the Son of Man comes under the control of the wicked.[177] There may be an allusion to those Psalms which speak of the hands of the wicked and the need for rescue from them (e.g. 36:12; 82:4; 140:8).[178] Wherever it comes from, however, it speaks to a presupposition of the guilt of the people to whom Jesus will be taken.[179]

Jesus's direction to his disciples, ἐγείρεσθε ἄγωμεν, cannot plausibly be a direction to run away, for the ensuing narrative depicts no desire for this on the part of Jesus and presents the disciples' abandonment as cowardly and embarrassing (particularly so for one individual, vv. 50–52).[180] Instead this indicates that in spite of his distress Jesus will actively meet the mob and expects his disciples to join him in doing so. On a practical level it could be that they are going to rejoin the other disciples in order that they be together when Judas arrives, especially so when compared with the earlier direction to sit and stay.[181]

This saying can also be seen as containing an AB-AB structure, where A has Jesus admonishing/directing his disciples (καθεύδετε τὸ λοιπὸν καὶ ἀναπαύεσθε· ἀπέχει· ἦλθεν ἡ ὥρα/ἐγείρεσθε ἄγωμεν) and B contains Jesus speaking of the Son of Man/himself facing betrayal (ἰδοὺ παραδίδοται ὁ υἱὸς τοῦ ἀνθρώπου/ἰδοὺ ὁ παραδιδούς με ἤγγικεν).

---

176. France, *Gospel of Mark*, 589; contra Stein, *Mark*, 665.
177. Marcus, *Mark*, 989.
178. Collins, *Mark*, 682; Evans, *Mark 8:27—16:20*, 417–18.
179. Gundry, *Mark*, 876; France, *Gospel of Mark*, 590.
180. France, *Gospel of Mark*, 590; Collins, *Mark*, 682–83.
181. See France, *Gospel of Mark*, 590; Focant, *According to Mark*, 591–92.

The Emerging Picture of the Son of Man (14:32–52)

This saying primarily functions as comment on the narrative. It is distressing and "paradoxical" that the one who is to condemn the wicked and save his chosen ones should be put into the hands of sinners, but entirely consistent with Jesus's predictions and the inverted honor expected of the Son of Man (cf. 10:45).[182] Jesus declares that this auspicious time has finally come and predicts the imminent arrival of his betrayer (who does arrive immediately). Stressed as he was, Jesus appears completely resolved to go along with what he expects to take place.

This adds a slight nuance to the prediction of 9:31 where εἰς χεῖρας ἀνθρώπων has been replaced with "the more loaded phrase εἰς τὰς χεῖρας τῶν ἁμαρτωλῶν."[183] Since Judas arrives with those from the chief priests, scribes, and elders, Evans notes how, "Those who had criticized Jesus for associating with sinners are now themselves acting as sinners in the worst way. Sinful opposition to the person and ministry of the 'son of man' is thematic in the Markan Gospel."[184] Thus once again, rejection and conflict is very much on view in this Son of Man saying and it arises in the context of a rebuke of his disciples (cf. comments on 8:31).

Mark 14:53–65

The Scene (14:53–65)

The final Son of Man saying comes in Jesus's appearance before the Sanhedrin. This may not have been a formal trial, but rather "a kind of preliminary hearing to determine if Jesus was as dangerous as the leadership sensed and whether he could be sent credibly for judgment by Rome."[185] Whether formal or not, one might expect that a group as concerned with propriety as the Sanhedrin would follow reasonable processes, but as the narrator makes clear, there is little in the way of due process and justice: false witnesses offer inconsistent testimony (v. 56) and council members are hoping to condemn Jesus (v. 55). Jesus does not respond to the false witnesses, even when he is given a direct opportunity (vv. 60–61a). He does respond however to the high priest's question: "Are you the Christ, the Son of the Blessed One?" and his response contains the Son of Man statement.

---

182. Marcus, *Mark*, 989–90.
183. France, *Gospel of Mark*, 589–90.
184. Evans, *Mark 8:27—16:20*, 417–18.
185. Bock, "Blasphemy," 64.

Jesus's statement elicits anguish, condemnation, and violence. The anguish is evidenced in the high priest tearing his clothes (cf. Gen 37:34; 2 Sam 13:19), which is in line with a response to blasphemy expected by the Mishnah (m. Sanh. 7:5).[186] The condemnation is evident in his rhetorical question about whether more witnesses are needed and the declaration of blasphemy. His pronouncement is unanimously confirmed by the council and they agree to the sentence of death (v. 64). People in the group and the officers begin to act in violence intended primarily to shame Jesus: spitting, punching, and slapping. All this matches the pattern of Jesus's predictions from earlier in the narrative (esp. 10:33–34).

The Saying (14:62)

Jesus's answer to the high priest is emphatic and direct: Ἐγώ εἰμι. It might just be possible that this statement offers some hint of a divine claim, but it most likely gives a simple affirmative answer to the question asked. Given the accusations made about his claims of authority over the temple, the high priest asked, in accordance with 2 Samuel 7:12–14, "If Jesus is the promised Davidic Messiah, who is God's son?" Jesus publicly accepts that this is who he claims to be, so clearly the time for any secrecy concerning his identity as the Christ is concluded.[187]

Jesus, however, does not stop with the affirmation but promises that they will see the Son of Man. Marcus is correct to point out that "Jesus does not explicitly claim to be the Son of Man he describes here, but the high priest has asked him . . . and the high priest's ensuing charge of blasphemy probably picks up not only Jesus' implicit affirmation of his divine sonship but also what he says about the Son of Man's elevation to God's right hand."[188] Jesus promises that the council members will—in the future—witness his glory and since what Jesus speaks of even surpasses what they might have expected of the Messiah, they decide that this is blasphemy. His mention of seeing the Son of Man (ὄψεσθε τὸν υἱὸν τοῦ ἀνθρώπου) alludes to Daniel 7, but what follows contains what many commentators see as a combination of Daniel 7 and Psalm 110.[189]

---

186. Evans, *Mark 8:27—16:20*, 452–53; Focant, *According to Mark*, 607–8; Marcus, *Mark*, 1008.

187. France, *Gospel of Mark*, 610.

188. Marcus, *Mark*, 1007.

189. Evans, *Mark 8:27—16:20*, 451–52; France, *Gospel of Mark*, 611–13; Edwards, *Gospel*, 447; Focant, *According to Mark*, 607; Stein, *Mark*, 684–85; Collins, *Mark*, 704–5.

Firstly, the Son of Man will be seen ἐκ δεξιῶν καθήμενον τῆς δυνάμεως. Jesus appears to match the high priest's circumlocution (ὁ εὐλογητός) with his own ἡ δύναμις, though it should be noted that the origins of Jesus's choice of term are "strongly debated."[190] The vision sounds very similar to what the Psalmist saw, "The Lord says to my Lord: 'Sit at my right hand until I make your enemies a footstool for your feet.'"

Secondly, and very clearly alluding to Daniel, he will be seen ἐρχόμενον μετὰ τῶν νεφελῶν τοῦ οὐρανοῦ. How the Son of Man can be simultaneously "sitting" and "coming" is not difficult to explain if the Son of Man is sitting in a cloud-chariot like that of Ezekiel 1.[191] Indeed, God's chariot in Ezekiel 1 has a high throne on it and the one seated on it is something like a human (Ezek 1:26). Stein suggests that this is the resurrection and ascension (sitting) followed by his return (on the clouds),[192] but his account fails to explain how those in the Sanhedrin could witness the former event. Since the statement is clearly visionary and apocalyptic the events need not be interpreted quite so literally or in sequence,[193] but they should be seen as a statement about the eschatological vindication of Jesus.

Interpreted in line with the context of Psalm 110 and Daniel 7, Jesus is implying that the Christ, the Son of Man, is promised to, respectively, have enemies underfoot and authority to judge all. Combining these passages together in his answer, "Jesus both affirms his divine Sonship before the high priest and portrays himself as the fulfiller of the eschatological mission of the Son of Man. . . . Though Jesus is dishonored by the high priest, he will be honored by God; and in place of his present vilification, God will vindicate the Son."[194] Thus the point of Jesus's answer is to warn the high priest and the council about the way that they are responding to him,[195] as he once warned his disciples about being ashamed of his words: "likewise the Son of Man will be ashamed of him when he comes in the glory" (8:38).

---

190. See discussion in Focant, *According to Mark*, 610; Marcus, *Mark*, 1008.

191. Evans, *Mark 8:27—16:20*, 452.

192. Stein, *Mark*, 684-85.

193. That is, "sitting at the right hand of power" may be entirely euphemistic for having a supreme authority, and the two participial clauses may be interpreted as a hendiadys.

194. Edwards, *Gospel*, 447.

195. Contra Collins, *Mark*, 705.

The Emerging Picture of the Son of Man (14:53–65)

This final Son of Man saying offers a public confirmation in the most emphatic terms of Jesus's expectation regarding his future. It serves as the culmination of a number of themes already witnessed in Mark's Gospel.[196] In regard to present authority, Jesus plainly accepts the designations of the Christ and the Son of God in the moment. In then switching the appellative to Son of Man, a direct link between the Messiah and the Son of Man is confirmed. Jesus then points to the full and final revelation of himself as the Son of Man presented as both the "Lord" of Psalm 110 and the one "coming in the clouds" in Daniel's vision. As in 13:26–27, he has a power and authority equal with the divine and eschatological vindication in the fullest possible terms. The relationship between the Old Testament Scriptures and the Son of Man is also confirmed. As the first Son of Man saying resulted in a quiet accusation of blasphemy from some scribes, this final saying results in the unanimous agreement of the entire Sanhedrin that in speaking this way Jesus is placing himself on a level with God and is deserving of death. Thus, the authority (both present and eschatological) and the imminent death of the Son of Man reach their climax through this episode, while links with Messiah, Scripture and conflict-rejection are confirmed.

---

196. Though this paragraph could be more filled out, the following chapter will comment on what has been explored throughout this chapter.

4

Synthesis of the Markan Son of Man

THE EXEGETICAL WORK ABOVE leads to a number of conclusions regarding the nature of the Son of Man as presented by Mark's Gospel. Firstly, though not always quoted in direct speech, it is always used by Jesus to refer exclusively to himself in serious sayings about his ministry and coming. Conversely, there is no association of ὁ υἱὸς τοῦ ἀνθρώπου with anyone else's speech or vocation, nor is it used by Jesus in mundane statements about his situation. This makes describing the phrase quite complex. On the one hand, it cannot be a simple circumlocution for "I."[1] On the other hand, calling Son of Man a "title" appears inadequate since there is so little evidence for an existing Son of Man expectation and that "it has not been changed into a Christological title appears from the inevitable fact that it never turns up in the Gospels in confessional sayings, much as it is never employed in a predicative way."[2] A way forward may be to consider Son of Man a kind of self-chosen honorific which functions in a way similar to Novenson's examination of Paul's use of Χριστός.[3] Jesus may well have used this phrase in such a way that it came to express his "inalienable uniqueness" and thus through Mark's record of it "the unmistakable uniqueness of Jesus is emphasised."[4] Broadhead describes Mark's use of Son of Man as "a mysterious but valid description which belongs appropriately to the mission

---

1. So also Burkett, *Son of Man Debate*, 84.
2. Müller, *Expression Son of Man*, 419.
3. Novenson, *Christ among the Messiahs*, esp. ch. 3.
4. These quotes, cited by Novenson, were made regarding Χριστός in Paul respectively by Hengel, "'Christos' in Paul," 74; and Grundmann, "Χριστός in Paul's Epistles," 9:540.

and identity of Jesus."[5] Jesus's appellative use of Son of Man could thus be considered as something of a nickname which only Jesus used for himself to capture his position and actions in the present, in the imminent future, and in the eschaton.

Secondly, this leads to the three broad categories of time raised in the Son of Man sayings and the ideas associated with them. The first of these phases deals with the *present* and conveys the idea of *supreme authority* presented so clearly in 2:10 and 2:28, though also touched on in 9:9 (after the transfiguration) and 10:45 (since the Son of Man is presented as the servant leader par excellence). The Son of Man on earth has divine prerogatives. The second phase is the *imminent* fate of handing over, condemnation, suffering, death, and resurrection. This is most clearly presented in the "passion predictions" of 8:31, 9:31–32 and 10:33–34. It is touched on by 9:9 (which speaks of resurrection and thus assumes death) and in doing so presumes the fulfillment of the prediction. An interpretation of the Son of Man's actions is provided by 10:45 and 14:20–21 (this latter when read in context of the Last Supper)—the Son of Man's death is a sacrifice which achieves a redemption for God's people. This "imminent suffering" theme begins to be played out in 14:41–42 and 14:62, but it should be noted that it concludes not with Jesus's death but with the resurrection. In the third phase, the Son of Man will come in an eschatological theophanic glory—"even equal to that of the Father,"[6] gather his elect and be ashamed of those who were ashamed of him (8:38; 13:26–27; 14:62). Though there is a general progression from one phase to the next in Mark's story, this is not strict and the Gospel places ideas together within the same episode which would indicate that these are not three distinct "Son of Man" concepts tracked onto one person, but one "Son of Man" person with three roles to play at different times.

Thirdly, the public association of the term ὁ υἱὸς τοῦ ἀνθρώπου with Jesus, even before his death, let alone his final coming, makes the Markan presentation very distinct from that of the Similitudes whose Son of Man is unknown until the final revelation. Further, Jesus appears more comfortable speaking about himself as the Son of Man in more public settings, than he is at accepting renown for his miracles and the designation Christ (cf. 1:44; 5:43; 8:30–31; with 2:10; 2:28; 8:38; 14:62—though in this last example he publicly admits he is the Christ). That said, the majority of the Son of Man sayings are presented to the disciples in private, especially those that relate to his immediate suffering, death, and resurrection. The Son of Man's action

---

5. Broadhead, *Naming Jesus*, 131.
6. Grindheim, *God's Equal*, 204.

in using authority to serve, and enduring suffering before experiencing glory becomes a pattern for the disciples to emulate (esp. 8:31–38; 10:45). In Mark's story then, it appears that although Jesus was comfortable referring to himself publicly as the Son of Man, he was very keen to make sure that his disciples understood that the one with supreme present authority who will eventually come in divine glory is the same one who will suffer betrayal and death and then rise after three days. That is why he set aside significant time to teach the disciples privately on this matter.

Finally, there are three additional themes linked with the Son of Man in Mark's Gospel. Each of these themes relates to sayings from each of the time categories above, and thus can be said to offer further unity to the Son of Man concept itself. These are, firstly, the association with Old Testament prophecy and expectation, secondly, the link between the Messiah and the Son of Man, and thirdly, the conflict and rejection of the Son of Man, especially by the Jewish leaders. The final theme—of conflict and rejection—is evident in every Son of Man episode in Mark and thus could be thought of as the primary unifying theme.[7]

The theme of Old Testament prophecy is first clearly seen when Jesus appeals to 1 Samuel 21:1–9 to justify his "present authority" over the Sabbath in 2:23–28. The "imminent suffering and resurrection" of the Son of Man is described as "necessary" (8:31), according to what "is written" (9:12, 14:21; and cf. 14:49), and at a set time (14:41). There are strong links between the "suffering servant" of Isaiah and Mark 10:45, but scholars point to a range of passages that may possibly provide further background for the Son of Man's suffering. There are hints of reference to Daniel 7 early in the Gospel, but definitely so in 13:26–27 and 14:62 which speak of Jesus's eschatological coming. Mark 14:62 also alludes fairly clearly to Psalm 110. The link to Ezekiel is to be explored below, and other more tenuous links may be drawn and assessed, but what has been presented is sufficient to see the significance and relation of Old Testament prophecy to the Son of Man.

---

7. Contra Grindheim, who concludes, "The theme that unites all the sayings is the question of authority. The earthly Jesus demonstrates his authority (1); his authority is rejected, which leads to suffering (2); but his authority is vindicated and he returns in glory (3)." While this is a reasonable summary of the narrative and relates authority to the three categories, there are two issues that cause me to consider this conclusion suboptimal. Firstly, the rejection and suffering of (2) are antithetical to the kind of authority expressed in (1) and (3). Secondly, while antithesis can offer relationship, Grindheim's approach also appears to section off the resurrection from the suffering. In my analysis, I have suggested the relationship with Messiah and scriptural fulfillment are significant unifying themes and both carry with them strong ideas of authority in ways that do not require holding together antithetical concepts and maintain the categories described above distinctly. Grindheim, *Christology*, 58.

Jesus's appeal to 1 Samuel 21:1-9 likewise establishes the first definitive link between a messianic expectation and the Son of Man where Jesus speaks of his present authority. The exchange between Peter and Jesus in 8:29-31 joins the Christ with the theme of the Son of Man and his imminent suffering and resurrection. In 8:38, Jesus speaks of the Son of Man as God's son and this, in keeping with 2 Samuel 7 and Psalm 2, is clearly messianic language being related to his final coming in glory. Moreover, in 14:62 Jesus affirms his identity as Christ and Son of the Blessed, before adding that the Son of Man would be seen in the superlative position of authority. This christological relationship is also evident in that kingdom language arises directly in 9:1 and 14:25, and it is also the presumed concept in the request of James and John (10:37) and the ingathering of 13:27.[8] Thus Mark's book leaves no doubt that the Messiah is the Son of Man and is Jesus.

The final unifying theme is that of conflict and rejection. Every Son of Man saying, when read in its episode, expects or portrays the Son of Man (and at times his elect) in a conflict with others. While significant opposition comes from the betrayer found among his disciples (esp. 14:20-21; 14:41-42), most often Jewish leaders are those who stand in opposition to the Son of Man (2:10; 2:28; 8:31; 9:12-13; 10:33; 14:62; and cf. also 13:9, 26). This theme and its unifying nature is perhaps most clearly seen through the bookending discussions of blasphemy whereby Jesus is accused and then condemned of a capital offence by religious leaders. The first comes quietly by some scribes just before Jesus's first Son of Man saying, and the last comes publicly by the Sanhedrin just after the final Son of Man saying.[9]

In conclusion, according to the Gospel of Mark, Jesus alone used ὁ υἱὸς τοῦ ἀνθρώπου to refer to himself and his present authority, imminent suffering and resurrection, and final glorification. Jesus's consistent and exclusive appellative use results in the term having the function of a self-chosen honorific or nickname. He used it publicly, but privately emphasized to his disciples the suffering and resurrection he was about to undergo, in part so that they could emulate his action. The Son of Man is the Messiah, the Son of God, and a descendant of David. The Son of Man shares divine

---

8. The Gospel of Mark has a serious concern with the kingdom of God, since it forms the basis of so much teaching (e.g. Mark 1:15; 4:1-34; 9:42-50; 10:13-31). Much of this kingdom focused material is outside the scope of this study, but this is mainly due to the limitations of the methodology employed, i.e. focusing on the episodes where Son of Man language is used. Further, more integrated study of the whole narrative of Mark may well find further links between Son of Man and the kingdom of God.

9. This conflict that the Son of Man faced from his own people was the primary impetus for the writing of this book and the reexamination of Ezekiel as a possible source for this Son of Man opposed by the people of Israel. Whether there is scope to examine Ezekiel as background for the Son of Man is the next topic for attention.

authority: able to forgive sins in the present and responsible for the execution of the final judgment. The Son of Man's fate is determined by the plans of God revealed in Scripture, with Daniel 7 preeminent among the passages referenced. The Son of Man is always in conflict, especially with the leaders of his own people.

5

Why Ezekiel Deserves Some Further Interaction

Having established a number of conclusions regarding the Son of Man in Mark's Gospel it is necessary to show why Ezekiel should even be considered as a possibility for the background of this phrase's form and meaning.

Reopening the Door

Daniel Burkett's "The Son of Man Debate," offers this evaluation of the possible link between Ezekiel's use of בֶּן־אָדָם and Jesus's use of ὁ υἱὸς τοῦ ἀνθρώπου:

> The theory that traces the Gospel "Son of Man" to Ezekiel has never been widespread and now appears only sporadically. Scholten criticized the idea that "Son of Man" identified Jesus as a prophet like Ezekiel, pointing out that Ezekiel was not called "son of man" on account of his prophetic office. Later scholars emphasized that the usage in Ezekiel cannot explain the distinctive features of the Gospel "Son of Man" sayings: "the Ezekielic hypothesis cannot explain the necessity of suffering in the predictions of the Son of man's passion even unto death, nor the august dignity of the Son of man in sayings portraying him as the heavenly witness or judge."[1]

Burkett, citing Higgins and also following Scholten, considers a background for the Gospels' Son of Man arising from Ezekiel as a fringe

---

1. Burkett, *Son of Man Debate*, 60; quoting Higgins, *Jesus*, 16; and citing Scholten, *Specimen*, 196.

view, unworthy of deeper attention. While a lack of scholarly interaction might indicate a topic lacks credibility, what Burkett discerns as "sporadic" scholarship might indicate that the topic has *not yet* been adequately explored. In contrast to Burkett, BDAG puts this alternative viewpoint in very strong terms during its discussion of the phrase ὁ υἱὸς τοῦ ἀνθρώπου: "Much neglected in the discussion is the probability of prophetic association suggested by the form of address Ezk 2:1 al. (like the OT prophet [Ezk 3:4–11] Jesus encounters resistance)."[2]

The portion of the quote above from Higgins points to some avenues for exploration, raising four questions: 1. On what grounds was Ezekiel called "son of man"? 2. What relationship did that designation have with his identity and role? 3. Would a relationship to Ezekiel help to explain Jesus's linking of Son of Man with his suffering and death? 4. Would it help to explain the authority of Jesus as a "heavenly witness or judge"? These questions will be dealt with in the following two chapters, but the short statement from BDAG itself suggests that there may be a much more positive answer to questions 1–3. The answer to them steps into the world of Old Testament research, rather than New Testament, and in the last fifty years there has been a large amount of research done on the book of Ezekiel, much of it after the "sporadic" and "occasional" scholarship to which Burkett refers to in his analysis which sought to link Ezekiel to the New Testament Son of Man. Contemporary critical scholarship in regard to the question of Ezekiel's presentation of "son of man" language should therefore be considered before accepting that Ezekiel could not offer some background for Jesus's use of Son of Man.

Danielic Background and Its Limitations

In suggesting that an Ezekielic background be considered, the Danielic background may be clarified and added to, but it cannot be denied. Based on the analysis presented in chapters 3 and 4, there can be no doubt that Daniel 7 offers a significant, though not exhaustive, background source for the Son of Man motif in Mark's Gospel. Jesus makes a very clear reference to Daniel's night vision.

Daniel itself, however, has a relationship with the book of Ezekiel. On the relationship between the books themselves Daniel Block writes, "One may recognize Ezekiel's literary influence in the apocalyptic writings of Daniel."[3] Widder comments, "Most closely related to the fiery scene before

2. BDAG, s.v. "υἱός," γ. ὁ υἱὸς τοῦ ἀνθρώπου.
3. Block, *Ezekiel*, 43.

Daniel [in 7:9–14] is Ezekiel's vision of the divine chariot. The chariot of Ezekiel 1 also had blazing wheels, and from its fiery cloud emerged four fiery creatures, a small council of beings accompanying Yahweh. In Daniel's vision there are thrones for the council members, though only one fiery throne with thousands of other heavenly beings attending the one on it."[4] These are just two among many scholars to point to the similarity in form and function of Ezekiel's and Daniel's visions of God and suggest a degree of dependency.[5] "The visions of Ezekiel are of great importance," writes Collins. "The influence of these passages on Daniel 8–12 is obvious."[6] Moving to a discussion of "son of man" phrasing in Daniel, some scholars also find background in Ezekielic imagery and phrasing. There are a number of scholars who suggest that the one "like a son of man" (Dan 7:13) might be specifically drawn from Ezekiel's inaugural vision of one on the throne who looks human (Ezek 1:26).[7] This fits well with the authority afforded the human-like person riding on the clouds.[8] It does not, however, offer a reasonable explanation for Daniel's divergence in phrase selection, especially considering the way in which בֶּן־אָדָם is used throughout the rest of Ezekiel. Harman and Di Lella thus point to Ezekiel 2:1 for that phrasing. "[T]he Aramaic term . . . may have been used here under the influence of the Book of Ezekiel, where the corresponding Hebrew term . . . is frequently used by God in addressing the prophet."[9] The following chapter, Daniel 8:17, is the only place, outside Ezekiel, where a prophet is addressed as בֶּן־אָדָם. By this point in Daniel's work, the language has switched from Aramaic to Hebrew and the referent of the figure has changed from the eschatological judge of a vision to Daniel himself. Eichrodt states that Daniel 8:17 is derived from Ezekiel 2:1 to express "the weakness of the creature to whom the mighty Lord shows such condescension."[10] Thus in the night vision of chapter 7 and in the chapter following, the book of Daniel demonstrates strong affinity to the Ezekielic ideas generally and perhaps also to "son of man" phrasing specifically. These need further scholarly exploration and evaluation,

---

4. Widder, *Daniel*, 155–56.

5. Others include Steinmann, *Daniel*; Pace, *Daniel*; Hartman and Di Lella, *Book of Daniel*; Miller, *Daniel*.

6. Collins, *Daniel*, 306.

7. These authors are by no means uniform in their reasoning or in the confidence of their suggestion: Kanagaraj, *Mysticism*, 172–73; Collins, *Hermeneia*, 306; Schmidt, "Son of Man," 22; Rowland, *Open Heaven*, 94–104, 182.

8. Steinmann, *Daniel*, 328–29, 339–40.

9. Hartman and Di Lella, *Book of Daniel*, 218.

10. Eichrodt, *Ezekiel*, 61; Hartman and Di Lella, *Book of Daniel*, 85–86; Block, *Ezekiel*, 30.

but it seems that a number of Old Testament scholars are quite convinced that there is some dependence of Daniel on Ezekiel around this vision of the heavenly court and the language of "son of man." Daniel presents his material in similar ways and utilizes Ezekielic turns of phrase at least once or twice. If Jesus alludes to Daniel and Daniel depends on Ezekiel, then the Son of Man that the Gospels present, in some respect, draws on Ezekiel.

Critically, major themes of ὁ υἱὸς τοῦ ἀνθρώπου in Mark's Gospel included suffering and rejection especially from the Jewish leadership and this is difficult to find in Daniel 7. While there might be a plausible link to suffering in Daniel 7 through the relationship between the "one like a son of man" and "the saints of the Most High" who are oppressed by their enemies (Dan 7:21, 25),[11] there is not any sense of a rejection of the "son of man" by the Jewish people—in fact, in context, the only mention of the Israelites is as the saints, the faithful remnant of the Jewish people. Thus, the Danielic background fails to provide grounding for this critical aspect of the Son of Man.

It is of course possible that Jesus simply invented this aspect of Son of Man, but that would fail to account for his consistent teaching that the Son of Man would be rejected and suffer according to God's plans revealed in Scripture. Indeed, the idea that there might be more background than that which arises from Daniel 7 is canvassed by some scholars. A number suggest that elements from the Psalms (especially Pss 22; 69; 118:22) and the Servant Songs of Isaiah (especially Isa 52:13—53:12) are combined with Danielic concepts (of authority and eschatological judgment) and, of course, the Danielic phrasing of Jesus's Son of Man.[12] Howard Marshall comments, "not surprisingly, motifs from several OT passages which were regarded as providing the pattern for the destiny of Jesus are coalesced to give a picture of him as the suffering, vindicated and authoritative Son of man."[13] The point of this book is not to explore the veracity of these broader claims, but if a wider background for Jesus as Son of Man is to be considered then why not Ezekiel?

---

11. Though it should be noted that there is by no means a consensus on the precise nature of the relationship between the saints and the "son of man" in Daniel.

12. E.g. France, *Gospel of Mark*, 359–60; Marcus, *Mark*, 645; Van Iersel, *Mark*, 300; Collins, *Mark*, 430–31; Gundry, *Mark*, 485.

13. Marshall, "Son of Man," 776.

Awareness of Ezekiel and Hebrew Language

Two serious reasons for rejecting an Ezekielic background for ὁ υἱὸς τοῦ ἀνθρώπου can be considered and refuted. Firstly, some have argued that Hebrew was already only a literary language by the first century. Casey's work in particular has argued that of the four languages Jesus may have spoken, namely Latin, Greek, Hebrew, and Aramaic, Aramaic was far and away the most likely language. It was the *"lingua franca,"* he claims, for Jews "in Israel at the time of Jesus."[14] This would make any Hebrew, and therefore Ezekielic, background less direct and this has flow-on effects for the veracity of the Greek of the New Testament in transmission and translation.[15] The second reason relates simply to whether Ezekiel was well known in the New Testament era. It must be admitted that there is scant evidence regarding quotation of, allusion to, or some other dependence upon, Ezekiel within the Synoptic Gospels.[16] Verbal dependence on Ezekiel is minimal in the New Testament, with only five examples, three from Revelation (Rev 1:15; 10:10; 18:1),[17] and two from 2 Corinthians 6:16–17. There are only five (excl. parallels) examples that demonstrate some Ezekielic influence in the Synoptic Gospels (Mark 6:34; 4:3; 8:18; Luke 1:52; 13:19; 19:10).[18] Both the awareness of Hebrew and awareness of Ezekiel itself will now be demonstrated.

Lukaszewski, in his assessment of the *Vorlage* of ὁ υἱὸς τοῦ ἀνθρώπου, has shown that the matter of language is not as simple as Casey makes out.[19] Latin, though still an unlikely candidate, was used by some Jews who worked in Roman households. Koine Greek had been an administrative language since the time of Alexander and so "the likelihood of Jesus being conversant with and even teaching in Greek is quite high."[20] Hebrew was certainly a literary language, but it was the language of Judaism and

---

14. Casey, *Solution*, 116.

15. Consider this argument from Evans as an example of how Ezekiel might be dismissed on language grounds: "Christensen (*ST* 10 [1956] 1–24) appeals to *Tg*. Ezek 12:1–16 as attesting an interpretive scriptural background to Jesus' words. However, there really is little in this passage, either in Hebrew or Aramaic (or Greek), that substantiates this proposal. Even the epithet "'son of man' in *Tg*. Ezek 12:2 is בר אדם *bar ʾādām*, not בר אנוש *bar ʾĕnôš*. Thus, the one essential element is missing." Evans, *Mark 8:27—16:20*, 377.

16. Though significant work has been done in regard to John's Gospel, e.g. Vawter, "Ezekiel and John," 450–58; Manning, *Echoes of a Prophet*; Peterson, *John's Use of Ezekiel*; Ellens, *Son of Man*, 141–44.

17. Bullock, "Ezekiel," 23; citing Vanhoye, "Ézéchiel."

18. Bullock, "Ezekiel," 23, following Nestlé.

19. Lukaszewski, "Issues."

20. Lukaszewski, "Issues," 15.

was spoken in Judea until the Mishnaic period. "Given the aforementioned language candidates, any attempt to unearth the Aramaic source behind ὁ υἱὸς τοῦ ἀνθρώπου must first justify why an Aramaic source—as opposed to Hebrew or Greek—is necessary."[21]

The Greek, ὁ υἱὸς τοῦ ἀνθρώπου, has no equivalent anywhere else in extant contemporary literature, but the lexemes are completely natural in Greek, so too the grammar, especially by the time of the New Testament.[22] Just because it may be odd Greek does not mean it is non-Greek.[23] The Semitic influence behind ὁ υἱὸς τοῦ ἀνθρώπου can only ever be realized by its comparison with Semitic literature known at the time and its religious overtones. Jesus's singular double articular phrase may simply be a Semitism which existed only in Greek, but an Aramaic or Hebrew *Vorlage* also seems quite possible.[24]

With regard to a Hebrew *Vorlage*, Lukaszewski notes that there is not enough known about the grammar and syntactical development of Hebrew in first-century Judea to make a judgment in either direction. Within his analysis, Lukaszewski also makes a number of points pertinent to the questions at hand in this chapter. Since Jesus quotes the Old Testament, he shows himself "quite conversant with Hebrew, preferring it over any Aramaic paraphrase."[25] Additionally he points out that even if the phrase originates in Galilean Aramaic, it "was formalized in [Hebrew] Judea."[26] "Consequently, one cannot rule Hebrew out of the linguistic milieu behind the Son of Man sayings."[27] The wider argument will not seek to ascertain nor argue for a Hebrew *Vorlage*, as it is merely seeking to explore Ezekielic thought-background for the phrase, but the possible existence of such a *Vorlage* shows how direct the link may actually be.

Aramaic remains the most likely candidate for the original language of the sayings. But Lukaszewski concludes that, though a touchstone for Aramaic grammar and syntax has been provided through Qumran, there remains so much more work to be done both in Aramaic and the other languages such that "no further clarification seems possible with respect

---

21. Lukaszewski, "Issues," 16.

22. The pattern article–noun-(genitive-article)-(genitive-noun) is found across the New Testament.

23. Lukaszewski, "Issues," 25.

24. Lukaszewski, "Issues," 26. Lukaszewski also notes pre-Arabic dialects as a possibility, but there is not enough extant material to move forward with this option.

25. Lukaszewski, "Issues," 19.

26. Lukaszewski, "Issues," 19.

27. Lukaszewski, "Issues," 19.

to a form, never mind a definition of an Aramaic Son of Man."[28] Even accepting that Aramaic was the primary language of Jesus and his apostles, and that the Son of Man sayings of the Gospels were originally given in Aramaic, does not in itself necessarily diminish the ability for the thought-background to come from Hebrew texts in general nor Ezekiel in particular. Further, given what is currently known about the linguistic milieu of first-century Palestine, while acknowledging the limitations of that knowledge, it is not difficult to conclude that the New Testament could easily have adequately communicated in Greek the phrase used by Jesus.[29]

Hebrew may well have been known, but what of Ezekiel's work? It should be straightforward to demonstrate that Ezekiel was well known at the time of Jesus and that the Gospel writers would have expected that their readers either had or could gain a familiarity with Ezekiel, which would mean that Ezekiel might plausibly have formed part of the background for the Son of Man sayings of the Gospels.

Firstly, the Hebrew canon, however it existed at the time, clearly included Ezekiel at the time of Jesus. Beckwith and Leiman have argued that the entire canon of the Jewish people was closed by the first century BC,[30] and cite Jesus's reference to the first and last martyrs of the canon as according with such a view (Luke 11:51; cf. Gen 4; 2 Chr 24:19–22). Kim, on the other hand, suggests one can only be confident of a Pharisaic canon which became the majority canon at the end of the first century, before being closed in the second century.[31] Whatever the contention regarding various books and their authoritative status, Ezekiel's authority appears to have had no known doubt. Importantly, subsequent canonical works demonstrate an awareness of Ezekiel, developing his proto-apocalyptic style (in the case of Daniel and Zechariah) and following his practice of specific dating of oracles (in the case of Zechariah and Haggai).[32]

Secondly, Ezekiel's literary influence on Jewish literature contemporary with Jesus is significant. Ezekiel is mentioned in Sirach (49:8), 4 Maccabees (18:17), and Josephus (*Ant.* 10.5.1).[33] There are also surviving fragments of the "Apocryphon of Ezekiel," a first-century BC Jewish document which

---

28. Lukaszewski, "Issues," 27.

29. Ong, *Multilingual Jesus*; Gleaves, *Did Jesus Speak Greek?*; Millard, *Reading and Writing*.

30. Beckwith, *Old Testament*; Leiman, *Canon*; Leiman, *Canonization*.

31. Lim, *Jewish Canon*, 178–88.

32. Block, *Ezekiel*, 43.

33. Block, *Ezekiel*, 43.

offers some insight into the doctrine of resurrection.³⁴ Though there are only very occasional direct references to the biblical text of Ezekiel at Qumran, their temple plans, Zadokite priesthood claims, throne chariot references, as well as the more general theology of God, his rebellious people, and the hope of a remnant show "that the book of Ezekiel was highly treasured in this community." ³⁵

Thirdly, there is a clear expectation from the Gospel authors that their readers would be familiar, or should become familiar, with the Jewish Scriptures. Since Mark's presentation is most relevant for the purposes of this book, the discussion will be limited to his work. Jesus refers to the Old Testament numerous times within Mark's Gospel. He answers his opponents and teaches his disciples by regular reference to and appeal to the authority of Old Testament works from across the canon—the Pentateuch (e.g. 7:9–10, 10:5–9), the prophets (both former, e.g. 2:25–26, and latter, e.g. 7:6–8; 11:17; 14:27) and the writings (e.g. 12:36; 13:26; 14:34). Moreover, Jesus says "David spoke in the Holy Spirit" (12:36), and describes the Sadducees' error as arising because they "do not know the Scriptures or the power of God" (12:24). This is not only true of Jesus, for the beginning of the narrative shows that the Jesus of this Gospel is to be seen as the fulfillment of Scripture (1:1–3). Mark's frequent use of the LXX demonstrates the confidence placed in that translation, yet the use of Hebraic form at 14:34 demonstrates an awareness that the LXX is a translation of an underlying Hebrew. Thus, any faithful hearer of Mark's Gospel would be expected to read the Old Testament Scriptures in order to come to a mature understanding of Jesus, and Ezekiel can be included as a possible background for the Markan Son of Man.

The concerns regarding awareness of the Hebrew language and Ezekiel's work can thus be put aside. Indeed, as Lukaszewski states, given Jesus's use of Hebrew Scripture "combined with the Son of Man sayings in Ezekiel, there is both a religious and linguistic framework on which to argue for a Hebrew background."³⁶

Singular and Definite Son of Man

Even for readers familiar with the LXX, replete as it is with Semitic influence, the New Testament phrasing of Son of Man is surprising. There is no extant example of Greek, Hebrew, or Aramaic articular (whether mono or

---

34. Block, *Ezekiel*, 43.
35. Block, *Ezekiel*, 42; see also Lust, "Ezekiel Manuscripts."
36. Lukaszewski, "Issues," 19.

dual) and singular "son of man" form outside of the Gospels and subsequent literature.[37] Yet, the Gospels use the singular, double article phrase—ὁ υἱὸς τοῦ ἀνθρώπου—eighty-one times (incl. par.). Scholars regularly comment on this issue in their discussion of the Son of Man problem and have various explanations for how this came about. Few, if any, however, point out the only singular *definite* usage in Greek which is definitely pre-NT: this is the vocative usage found ninety-three times in Ezekiel and once in Daniel 8:17, which makes up over half of all the examples of the forms of "son of man" in the LXX.

As stated above, Daniel's single use of the phrase is most likely based on Ezekiel's use (Ezek 2:1).[38] In Ezekiel's book, God *never* calls Ezekiel himself by his proper name, addressing him instead as "son of man" ninety-three times. This speech is always private between God and his prophet, and is recorded as direct speech, such that Ezekiel's work never uses "son of man" outside the vocative case. In neither Greek nor Hebrew does the vocative take an article, and while the form is not different in Hebrew but is in Greek, vocative forms are by nature definite since they refer to specific agents. Therefore, υἱὲ ἀνθρώπου is definite, despite being anarthrous.

Therefore, the only *original* example of a *definite singular* use of "son of man," prior to the Gospels, is in Ezekiel. The Gospels' different case form and use of it in public address is still significant, so this does not by any means prove that Ezekiel is the background for the use of the articular-singular phrase. It does however suggest that Ezekiel's work is a candidate at the least for some kind of philological background for ὁ υἱὸς τοῦ ἀνθρώπου.

Conclusion

There can be little doubt that the presentation of the Son of Man in Mark's Gospel is meant to depend upon Daniel, but the gap between the Danielic "one like a son of man" and the Gospel's ὁ υἱὸς τοῦ ἀνθρώπου, especially on the issue of suffering and conflict with leaders of Israel, makes the possibility of an additional background worth exploring. Both Hebrew language and the book of Ezekiel were sufficiently well known at the time of Jesus to have plausibly contributed to the background for Jesus's use of the phrase.

---

37. Hurtado offers a good summary of these issues but overlooks Ezekiel's usage as an example of a definite singular. This is most likely due to a search being done on the basis of the article, overlooking the fact that a true vocative form will almost certainly lack an article, but remains definite nonetheless. Hurtado, "Summary."

38. See above, so Eichrodt, *Ezekiel*, 61; Hartman and Di Lella, *Book of Daniel*, 85–86; Block, *Ezekiel*, 30.

Moreover, the composition of Mark's Gospel demonstrates that Christians were expected to become familiar with the Jewish Scriptures at least in translation. The book of Ezekiel was a part of whatever can be considered the canon at the time. Thus, Mark's readers could be expected to explore Ezekiel, at least in translation, for an understanding of the phrase. The fact that the only singular definite usage in Greek outside of the New Testament is found in Ezekiel and Ezekiel-dependent Daniel, as well as the fact that these offer the only other example of the phrase being used as an appellative, offer further weight to the case for consideration. Thus, although there has been some examination of "son of man" concepts from Ezekiel which has not yielded consistent or widely received results for questions raised by the Son of Man problem, the time has come for a reappraisal making use of modern Ezekiel scholarship and this will be taken up in the remaining chapters.

6

Ezekiel's בֶּן־אָדָם

Introduction

THIS CHAPTER ATTEMPTS TO answer two significant questions: firstly, "what is בֶּן־אָדָם as a form of address intended to convey?," and secondly, "what is the effect of Ezekiel being addressed as בֶּן־אָדָם throughout the book?" The difference between the two questions hinges on the idea that were Yahweh, in Ezekiel's book, to address Ezekiel from time to time as "son of man," or even frequently as such, then it may offer nothing more than a regular use of the normal connotation of the phrase. However, in Ezekiel, uniquely among the prophets, God never calls Ezekiel by his proper name; instead he always calls him "son of man" and he does so ninety-three times. Bullock concludes that "the use of the title impresses a particular stamp on Ezekiel's ministry."[1] While "title" may not be the most appropriate designation for the phrase, the point of the second question in this chapter is to explore the impression created by that "particular stamp."

What Does בֶּן־אָדָם Convey?

In his commentary on Daniel, Steinmann comments that the Hebrew, as opposed to the Aramaic, use of "son of man" language is "in contexts that stress sinfulness, mortality, and frailty, which are the opposite of the characteristics of the Son of Man portrayed in Dan 7:13–14."[2] This view accords

---

1. Bullock, "Ezekiel," 28.
2. Steinmann, *Daniel*, 168–69; contra Moule, *Essays*, 75–90.

well with those translations which have sought to render the sense of the idiom (rather than opting for a word-for-word rendering) with the concept of "mortality" (e.g. TEV, NRSV, LEB n.,) or "humanity" (e.g. NCV, NIV2011 n., NET n.). Of these two options, given that the prophet's death is nowhere mentioned in the book,[3] most scholars would consider the latter more accurate.[4] The point of calling Ezekiel בֶּן־אָדָם is to place Ezekiel firmly among the category of humanity as opposed to the glorious divinity of Yahweh. As Block points out, this distinction is seen prominently in "Balaam's classic expression of the divine-human distinction in Num. 23:19: 'God (ʾēl) is not man (ʾîš) that he should lie;/Nor a son of man (ben-ʾādām) that he should change his mind.'"[5] It also accords well with the use of the phrase in Psalm 8, where in response to having considered the majesty of Yahweh on earth (v. 2) and in heaven (vv. 3, 4), the psalmist is surprised by his concern for humanity—מָה־אֱנוֹשׁ כִּי־תִזְכְּרֶנּוּ וּבֶן־אָדָם כִּי תִפְקְדֶנּוּ (Ps 8:5). Thus, while not necessarily implying death, בֶּן־אָדָם conveys a sense of mere humanity and fragility to Ezekiel.

Additionally, calling Ezekiel בֶּן־אָדָם singles him out from among his contemporaries, while clearly not set above them, since he remains only human. He is a particular בֶּן־אָדָם. The contrast to his people is most sharply seen in Ezekiel's commissioning (chs. 2–3). After chapter 1 has clearly envisioned the unrivalled glory of the all-powerful, all-mobile Yahweh, chapter 2 offers a long and deliberate report of Ezekiel's commissioning as Yahweh's prophet. The people he is sent to are described variously as rebellious (2:3), stubborn (2:4), hard (3:8), and unwilling to listen (3:7). They are not, however, foreigners, but his own nation, the Israelites, a fact which is emphatic in the commission (3:4–7). They, like their forefathers (2:3), will reject both Yahweh and his prophet (3:7). By contrast, Ezekiel is presented as fully under the control of Yahweh. Ezekiel is instructed to stand, and the Spirit overwhelms him and causes him to stand (2:1, cf. 3:24). Should there be any risk regarding the hardness of the rebellious people diminishing Ezekiel's obedience in speaking to them, of whether they listen or not, Yahweh promises to make Ezekiel himself obstinate—even harder than flint (3:9). Moreover, Yahweh instructs Ezekiel not only to speak his words, but to remain in his home without speaking until such time as Yahweh opens his mouth

---

3. Though perhaps there is a sense of death in Ezekiel falling on his face (1:28), only to be revived by the word and spirit of God (2:1–2), and this may fit with the theme of death and resurrection of the nation in the book (cf. esp. 37:1–14). Gowan, *Prophetic Books*.

4. Block, *Ezekiel*, 30–31; Bullock, "Ezekiel"; Duguid, *Ezekiel*, 71–73; Haag, "בֶּן־אָדָם"; Brownlee, *Ezekiel*, 25–26.

5. Block, *Ezekiel*, 30, n. 48.

to speak (3:24–27). Thus, Ezekiel will only speak what the Lord Almighty says, when he allows it, and where he allows it. At each point of instruction, the Spirit, or the hand of Yahweh, or divine promise, coincides with and drives the command to its completion.[6] Particular emphasis is made of Ezekiel's responsibility to declare the warnings of Yahweh (3:16–21), and yet 3:27 suggests that Ezekiel will not fail to speak when Yahweh opens his mouth. There is no contradiction in saying on the one hand that Ezekiel "is a man totally under the control of the Spirit of Yahweh; only what God says and does matters," and, on the other hand, Ezekiel's "primary identification is with his audience, not with the one who sent him."[7] From the moment he is first called בֶּן־אָדָם, Ezekiel is both placed among and against the בְּנֵי יִשְׂרָאֵל,[8] being commissioned and spiritually empowered to speak God's words to them in spite of their rebelliousness against God now being directed against him.[9]

The Effect of Calling Ezekiel בֶּן־אָדָם

Ezekiel is only referred to by his proper name at the very start of the book (1:1) and then in 24:24 (when Ezekiel is referred to within an oracle to be given to the people), and at all other times Ezekiel is referred to by personal pronouns and 93) בֶּן־אָדָם times). Given the autobiographical style of the book, it appears Ezekiel makes a deliberate choice to present the material in this way.[10] That is, he could have, without changing much of the core meaning of the oracles, ignored this form of address. Aside from reemphasising

---

6. Those imperatives are: to stand (2:2), to go to the Israelites (2:3; 3:4, 11), to not be afraid (2:6; 3:9), to speak Yahweh's words and warnings (2:7; 3:4, 11, 17, 27), to pay attention without rebellion (2:8; 3:10), to eat the scroll (2:8; 3:1, 3), to go to the valley (3:22) and to shut himself within his house (3:24). Take special note of the Hiphil with regard to eating and also the uncertainty about who binds Ezekiel.

7. Block, *Ezekiel*, 28, 31.

8. I don't mean to make too much of Son of Man/sons of Israel contrast, but the neat literary parallel could explain why Ezekiel chooses to use בְּנֵי יִשְׂרָאֵל in this instance. Chapter 3:5–6 shows just how similar and yet distinct Ezekiel is from his contemporaries. Dismissing בְּנֵי יִשְׂרָאֵל as always erroneous is mistaken and there is no textual reason to do so. As Block has it, "Ezekiel's partiality toward *bêt yiśrā' ēl* over *běnê yiśrā' ēl* should not be absolutized. . . . [The] prophet was free to use whichever expression was most appropriate for the context." Block, *Ezekiel*, 32. Contra Zimmerli, *Ezekiel* 2, 564.

9. For a similar discussion see Kanagaraj, *Mysticism*, 164.

10. At this point one might wish to distinguish between Ezekiel and his compiler/redactor, and in addition one could argue that having been addressed as such by Yahweh he had no choice but to convey it in this way. But these are beside the point for the rhetorical effect which I am discussing here.

his humanity, this reiteration leads the reader to the conclusion that Ezekiel, and no-one else, within this book at least, is בֶּן־אָדָם. בֶּן־אָדָם becomes tied to who Ezekiel is, what he is called to do, and then what he does. The specific application of this appellative for Ezekiel means that it becomes a kind of nickname that Yahweh uses for him.[11]

If this is to be considered a nickname, then it is a perplexing, complex, sort of nickname since Ezekiel himself remains a hidden figure in the book. Ezekiel discloses very little about his personal feelings in the book—only in 4:14; 9:8; 11:13; 21:5 (Eng 20:49); 24:24 (Eng v. 23); and 37:3 is there any insight into his reaction. Block rightly gets the sense that readers have "gained access to the private memoirs of a holy man" yet he "wonders if the real Ezekiel is ever exposed."[12] The nickname thus appears to relate, not to a characteristic of himself, but to the role which he fulfills as Yahweh's prophet. Ezekiel's book leaves the impression that whoever Ezekiel himself is, he is בֶּן־אָדָם: the word-of-Yahweh-directed, Spirit-controlled human.

This concept, that Ezekiel is the "בֶּן־אָדָם entirely controlled by Yahweh," is paramount for the rhetorical function of the book. For a group of people in the shame of exile with no access to Yahweh in his temple, but instead in the territory of Marduk, Ezekiel's work claims a commission from Yahweh who remains very high on his chariot throne. Ezekiel is the watchman on the wall, ready to warn the people about the grave future that awaits them (chs. 3, 33), but he is silent until he has words of such importance (e.g. 3:26–27; 33:22). His book then is not the words of a prophet who has received revelations from Yahweh from time to time, but who was otherwise able to speak and live freely. Rather Ezekiel *only* speaks Yahweh's words, at Yahweh's discretion by Yahweh's empowering. Calling Ezekiel בֶּן־אָדָם throughout the book reminds readers that, while human, he represents the all-powerful, all-mobile Yahweh described in the initial theophany (ch. 1), and every single thing Ezekiel says and does must be dealt with by his exilic audience as a matter of life and death.

Moreover, this בֶּן־אָדָם is not just the mouthpiece of Yahweh, but the actor for Yahweh. Aside from the various speech styles he employs, he is also, at various times, enacting the message and offering a sign to the people. He suffers the siege (ch. 4), his beard is shaved off (ch. 5), he goes into exile (ch. 12), he builds a road sign (ch. 24), the delight of his eyes is taken (ch. 24), he puts Judah and Ephraim back together (ch. 37). Duguid describes Ezekiel's role in delivering the message in action: "Ezekiel's proclamation is

---

11. While one might be tempted to call it an honorific, that would not convey the right tone, for calling him a human does not pay him some particular honour.

12. Block, *Ezekiel*, 27.

not delivered from the safety and comfort of an ivory tower but flows out of personal experience of the suffering of his people. Indeed, it may not be too strong to say that he has already ingested their suffering, in the form of the scroll covered with words of lament, mourning, and woe [i.e. in 2:8—3:3], just as in the temple ritual the priests would ingest the sin offering and thus absolve the guilt of the people."[13] Everything this בֶּן־אָדָם does and everything he says, even to his own detriment, will accord with Yahweh's revealed plans and purposes for him and for his people.

The role Ezekiel plays is nowhere more significant than when he becomes the agent of resurrection for the people of Israel in chapter 37, albeit within visionary experience. Throughout the vision Yahweh keeps his prophet actively involved. Ezekiel must declare the impossible command and promise of life to the exceedingly dry bones: הָעֲצָמוֹת הַיְבֵשׁוֹת שִׁמְעוּ דְּבַר־יְהוָה (vv. 4-6). Ezekiel speaks the prophecy commanded and is surprised by a rattling noise which starts with his prophesying (v. 7). This turns out to be the noise of the bones joining to one another. But while the bodies are restored there is still no breath/spirit within them (v. 8). So, in verse 9, Yahweh commands Ezekiel to prophesy to the Spirit to come and breathe into the killed ones (בהרוגים) to give them life. Again, Ezekiel prophesies as commanded (v. 10a, cf. 7a) and the dead rise as an exceedingly large army, חַיִל גָּדוֹל מְאֹד־מְאֹד. Renz questions the role of the prophet in the dry bones vision but this seems to have been done on the basis of the use of weqatal forms indicating a diminished role for the prophet (vv. 7a, 10a, 8a).[14] However, Ezekiel has a strong (seemingly idiosyncratic) preference for using weqatals and while they might in many cases move the material offline to the main narrative,[15] recent work on the verbal system might suggest that this is not a necessary implication.[16] Besides this, simply being offline to the main narrative would not in itself diminish the prophet's role in regard to his people. The power of the word does not come from him, but Ezekiel is not a *passive* observer. In the same valley where he was commissioned, given specific sign acts, and saw the temple vision (37:1; cf. 1:3; 3:22; 8:1),[17] "the prophet sees his work come to fruition."[18] He has

---

13. Duguid, *Ezekiel*, 70.

14. Renz, *Rhetorical Function*, 204-5.

15. E.g. Renz, *Rhetorical Function*, 204-6; Fox, "Ezekiel's Vision," 9; and Greenberg, *Ezekiel 21-37*, 747.

16. Athas and Young, *Elementary Biblical Hebrew*, 115-19.

17. Odell, *Ezekiel*, 451; Olley, *Ezekiel*, 236.

18. Odell, *Ezekiel*, 451.

an active and vital role to play within the vision,[19] even as he watches it unfold in awe,[20] and then in making it known to the Israelites. Secondly, and even if Ezekiel's role were marginalized, his work is still intended to have a positive effect among the exiles, and this is highlighted by this passage more than any other. In the vision, the prophet declares Yahweh's plans concerning bringing life to the bones, and this action moves the bones to become something better than before—bodies—though still dead. Then he is commanded to prophesy to the Spirit to bring life, and life is breathed into the people. Thus, when in verses 12–14, he speaks the plans of Yahweh to revive the people (who are the dry bones and see themselves as such [v. 11]), one would expect that his prophecy should have an effect. "The author thereby identifies the book of Ezekiel as a means to the transformation of Israel. What the prophet began to achieve through his ministry is to be completed through the book."[21] In the midst of hopelessness "readers are encouraged to make the vision of New Israel their own, since the transformation of their community is guaranteed through Yahweh's Spirit."[22] Yahweh used this בֶּן־אָדָם to promise judgment on the people (esp. chs. 8–11; 18) and all the nations (chs. 25–32), but makes him the agent of new life to a dead nation which, by his word and Spirit, becomes responsive to him.

It may even be appropriate to distinguish between Ezekiel as himself and as בֶּן־אָדָם, especially so if Daniel Block's theory regarding Ezekiel's resistance to his calling is correct. That is, the control placed on Ezekiel might arise out of a sense of reluctance on Ezekiel's participation as a prophet. Any risk that he might undermine the message of Yahweh when speaking of his own accord is thus entirely prevented. The best evidence for Ezekiel's resistance is the direct warning to be unlike the people in this regard (2:8) and the raging silence he had after the first vision (3:14–15). Block thus suggests, "The coming of the Spirit upon him is particularly reminiscent of the Spirit's activity in the book of Judges, when men were ill disposed toward doing the will of Yahweh."[23] This reluctant prophet theory is not without its critics. Ezekiel's immediate response to the theophany of chapter 1 is, after all, entirely appropriate and the Spirit's action in causing him to stand may have been necessary to allow a mere "son of man," however good, to gaze upon such glory. Ezekiel's response of silent rage might involve an amount of reluctance but may have had more to do with plain shock than

19. Cf. Duguid, *Ezekiel*, 427–28.
20. Greenberg, *Ezekiel 21–37*, 747.
21. Renz, *Rhetorical Function*, 250.
22. Renz, *Rhetorical Function*, 200.
23. Block, *Ezekiel*, 12.

hard-heartedness,[24] or perhaps even a kind of priestly seclusion.[25] Block's theory, however, does explain Yahweh's heavy-handedness with him (as Ezekiel himself put it in 3:14) and it might also accord with Ezekiel's theme of the end of false prophecy in Israel, along with the diminishing of human actors later in the book (most notably the king).[26] If Ezekiel was in some sense a rebellious prophet, then it means that this בֶּן־אָדָם is not only set against his own people in his commission, but even in some way against himself, making the relationship between this phrase and the theme of conflict with rebellious people very significant.

Even if the reluctant prophet theory is mistaken, the theme of conflict with his fellow Israelites and especially their leaders is quite pronounced as Ezekiel fulfills his commission to speak against the people of Israel throughout his book. He brings the whole community to trial and answers their attempts to wriggle free of responsibility (esp. ch. 18). In the vision of the renewed temple the people are no longer allowed to slaughter their own sacrifices (44:11), within the temple they are kept at a distance (40:29–31), and they are prevented from dwelling too close to the holy city as well (48:15–20). At various points he singles out those who have authority for particular mention, and the plan he lays out for the future of Israel shows how much needs to change in regard to them. The monarchy is attacked for its abuse of power and negligence (see esp. 33:22–24; 45:8). There will be a return to the godliness set by David in the future monarchy, but the title and the role are below what they once were (e.g. 34:23, he is an under-shepherd and is called נָשִׂיא). Though rarely mentioned directly, Ezekiel offers some significant critique of the priesthood. Ezekiel 22:26, in particular, offers serious criticism of the priests for their failure to apply properly the law relating to holiness, ceremonial cleanliness, and Sabbaths.[27] In Ezekiel 44 the whole community of Israel is criticized for their former practice (vv. 1–9) and the Levites are particularly singled out (v. 10), though still able to perform their role as temple guards, that is all (vv. 11–14). As a result, it is only the righteous Zadokites who are involved in the future cult (44:15). Ezekiel critiques false prophets and prophetesses for blocking and undermining his message and so leading the people of Israel astray (ch. 13). There is no mention of the prophets in the restoration of Israel. This might be expected, since, with

24. Whether because of what he had experienced, as in Greenberg, *Ezekiel 1–20*, 90; or at what his people were about to face, as in Duguid, *Ezekiel*, 70. Naylor thinks it combines shock and reluctance. Naylor, *Commentary*, 81, 86.

25. Odell, *Ezekiel*, 47.

26. See Duguid, *Leaders of Israel*.

27. Chs. 8–11 offer some strong cultic practice in Jerusalem, but priests are not particularly singled out as culpable for these problems (see below).

the exception of Ezekiel, the prophets addressed in the book are false prophets and one would not expect a restored covenant community to have false prophets. Ezekiel himself, however, takes on an incredibly significant role. Yahweh uses him to bring the word and the Spirit to the people (37:1–15), and then he is like a new Moses, receiving and passing on new plans for the place for meeting with God. While the whole community is held accountable and punished, Ezekiel singles out elders of the house of Israel and lay leaders (שָׂרֵי הָעָם, זִקְנֵי בֵית־יִשְׂרָאֵל) as particularly responsible for the abominable temple practices of chapter 8 and injustice in Jerusalem which leads to the departure of Yahweh's glory from its place, and the promise of the destruction of Jerusalem and its temple (e.g. 8:11–12; 11:1). In chapters 14 and 20 actual confrontation between the elders and Ezekiel takes place. Indeed, chapter 20 concludes with Ezekiel recording his frustration at their rejection of him as simply a teller of parables (20:49). Since the elders and lay leaders are not "shepherds" but among the sheep these must also be understood as the fat sheep of chapter 34. Like the false prophets, the lay leaders and elders gain no place in the restoration Ezekiel envisages. In sum, Ezekiel, through his book, condemns the people and leaders, and completely restructures every element of his community in his vision of chapters 40–48. Human leadership is quite regulated and restricted in the restored community, and all leaders, with the exception of himself and the Zadokite portion of the priesthood, face relegation and sometimes (as is the case for the elders and the false prophets) exclusion. Thus, a sharp conflict is evident between Ezekiel, the בֶּן־אָדָם, on the one hand, and the people, and especially their leaders, on the other.

Conclusion

In chapter 5, four questions were posed based on Higgins's conclusion about an Ezekielic Son of Man. The first two of those can now be answered: 1. On what grounds was Ezekiel called "son of man"? 2. What relationship did that designation have with his identity and role? Ezekiel was called בֶּן־אָדָם to emphasize his humanity as opposed to the divine initiator who called him, yet calling him בֶּן־אָדָם also singles him out as Yahweh's prophet for the rebellious people of Israel. The repeated used of this appellative puts a "particular stamp" on Ezekiel; it is a nickname which God uses for him and this is significant for the rhetorical function of the book. While Ezekiel himself is relatively undisclosed the reader is left with the impression that this בֶּן־אָדָם always and only speaks Yahweh's words and acts as his agent in various signs and visions, most strikingly in being the agent of the nation's resurrection. As this בֶּן־אָדָם, Ezekiel acts even at significant cost to himself, perhaps even against his own wishes. In fulfilling his commission the בֶּן־אָדָם of Ezekiel comes into sharp conflict with the Israelites and their leaders, especially the false prophets, the elders, and lay leaders. Though he proclaims the destruction of the temple in Jerusalem, in the end this book's בֶּן־אָדָם is like a new Moses, setting out the pattern for a new meeting place between Yahweh and his people.

Though not at all in accordance with the reluctant/rebellious prophet concept, Caragounis made similar observations to those above in his 1986 analysis and part of his conclusion is worth quoting at length:

> The cited cases amply show that the role which the prophet has assumed among his people is one of representative, intercessor and substitute. The appellation "son of man" is, therefore, not a characterization of him as a rebellious person, but is indicative of his identification with the wicked nation which he serves. Thus, the status of son of man is transferred from those to whom it properly belongs to the one who has identified himself with them and becomes their substitute. This transferred use of son of man in Ez is therefore a development of the concept . . . The appellation is no longer a descriptive designation, but a term denoting role or function. It introduces a new concept in Yahwism, whereby Yahweh's prophet-servant becomes identified with those to whom he channels God's message. He becomes a son of man in order to address sons of men.[28]

Both Caragounis and Porter (who recently drew significantly on his work),[29] notice that interpreters may have missed these concepts in Ezekiel and that perhaps "Ezekiel has more importance for discussion of the 'son of man' than has usually been thought."[30] They do not, however, go on to draw out the possible links with the Son of Man motif found in the Gospels. This is what will be done in the following chapter.

---

28. Caragounis, *Son of Man*, 60.
29. Porter, *Sacred Tradition*, 55–56.
30. Porter, *Sacred Tradition*, 55; citing Caragounis, *Son of Man*, 60.

7

Comparing the Ezekielic בֶּן־אָדָם to the Markan ὁ υἱὸς τοῦ ἀνθρώπου

THE TWO SONS OF man that have been discussed from Ezekiel and Mark's Gospel can now be compared. This chapter presents, in no particular order, points of similarity as well as dissimilarity. This chapter will raise possibilities but will leave the evaluation of these links and related issues (especially dependence) for the following chapter.

Points of Similarity

The first point to note in comparing these sons of man, was the philological link noted in chapter 5. Ezekiel's phrase is the earliest example of a singular definite form of "son of man." Its definiteness arises from being vocative, which does not take a different form in Hebrew, but does when translated to Greek (υἱὲ ἀνθρώπου); in neither language would it normally take an article as a vocative. It was heavily used throughout Ezekiel's work and almost certainly influenced Daniel's use of the phrase (Dan 8:17). The New Testament's ὁ υἱὸς τοῦ ἀνθρώπου is the original example of an articular, singular use of a "son of man" phrase in any extant language.[1] Thus there is an accordance of singular definite uses of a "son of man" phrase.

A second point of similarity is the use of a "son of man" phrase as a kind of nickname. In both instances the application is complex. In Mark's

---

1. As noted in chapter 5, Hurtado offers a good summary of these issues, but overlooks Ezekiel's usage as an example of a definite singular. This is most likely due to a search being done on the basis of the article, overlooking the fact that a proper Greek vocative form will almost certainly lack an article, but remains definite nonetheless. Hurtado, "Summary."

Gospel, Jesus uses it as a kind of self-prescribed honorific to capture his position and actions across his earthly life, his death and resurrection, and his role as eschatological judge. In Ezekiel's book, it is God's designation of the prophet used to emphasize his humanity while distinguishing him from his compatriots as the one bringing the word of Yahweh to them. Its repeated use, along with very little use of the prophet's real name and little disclosure of the prophet's own life and feelings, yields the result that his book is the product of the Spirit-controlled בֶּן־אָדָם. Though what is being conveyed by the nickname might be seen to differ in some important ways, using "son of man" as a nickname is unique to the works of Ezekiel and the Gospels.

A third point of comparison is that both instances link "son of man" with the themes of suffering, conflict, and rejection. One of the three categories for Jesus's Son of Man sayings was his imminent fate of rejection, suffering, and death before rising again. Moreover, even where the Son of Man saying itself conveys authority and eschatological judgment there is, in the context, almost always a link to conflict and rejection of him, most often by the Jewish leadership. Ezekiel's link to these ideas is likewise manifold. On its own, בֶּן־אָדָם, as a Hebrew idiom, frequently conveys frailty and humility. Ezekiel is commissioned to speak to a rebellious people, and he fulfills that commission by confronting and condemning the people along with their various leaders. With the exception of the Zadokite priests, the restoration of the temple sees the future leaders as diminished in their roles, while some (i.e. false prophets and the corrupt lay leaders) are excluded entirely. For their part the people and their leaders are dismissive of him (20:49). Furthermore, if, as Block suggests, Ezekiel should be thought of as a reluctant prophet and was thus restrained (not just enabled) by the Spirit from the time of his commission onwards, then the link between being called בֶּן־אָדָם and the theme of rejection might be even more pronounced. During his ministry Ezekiel himself has to eat the scroll of lament, lay siege to himself, pack and go into exile and even lose "the delight of his eyes." For both בֶּן־אָדָם and ὁ υἱὸς τοῦ ἀνθρώπου their interaction with their own compatriots brings them into serious conflict. Their compatriots misunderstand them and mock them. Both suffer among, and at times at the hand of, their fellow Israelites.

In doing so, both sons of men are also seen to be enacting divine plans and direction, which is a fourth point of similarity. From the point of his commission (and whether he was resisting or not) Ezekiel can only ever speak and act according to the revelation and enabling of Yahweh. Likewise, though not nearly as directly correlated, Jesus's three roles as Son of Man each fulfill some expectation derived from things written in Scripture. He appeals to his present authority by reference to King David, he speaks of his eschatological judgment by reference to Daniel and Psalm 110, and—most significantly of all—he goes to his death and resurrection at the set time and as it is written, likely drawing on Isaianic themes in 10:45. Jesus, like Ezekiel before him, fulfills the divine plan even though it causes great suffering.

Before long, however, as a fifth point of similarity, both sons of man are also vindicated. Though Ezekiel endures much through his ministry, he is given the privilege not only to speak of the promised return from exile and restoration of the kingdom, but he also becomes like a new Moses: laying out the temple plans for his people. Jesus's suffering is greater—extending to death itself—and so too is his vindication. ὁ υἱὸς τοῦ ἀνθρώπου is not only raised from the dead but given the divine authority to execute judgment on the wicked who were ashamed of him and rejected by him, while bringing salvation to his chosen ones who have remained faithful to him. The final pictures of both Ezekiel and Jesus point to authority and power for their respective son of man and also peace, security, and divine presence for those who respond to them appropriately.

A further motif connected to both Ezekiel and Jesus is that both share a role as predictors of the temple's destruction and as agents of the resurrection. Ezekiel's prediction of the temple's demolition would have been critical for his acceptance as a true prophet. His role as an agent for the resurrection of the nation is in the vision of chapter 37. Jesus predicts the destruction of the temple in Mark 13 (v. 2), in which he warns that those who remain loyal to him will be killed (vv. 9–13), but he says that following these things there will be a great theophany in which the Son of Man will come with great power and gather his elect. This gathering must include, therefore, even those who are dead. In predicting the temple's destruction both are quite similar—but there were other prophets who did the same. In predicting and being involved in a resurrection these two sons of men are unique. It should be noted however that Ezekiel's involvement is one of a vision and, in its immediate context, predicts the restoration of the geopolitical nation, not a literal resurrection. What Ezekiel does in vision as metaphor, Jesus predicts he will accomplish in actual history, indeed as history's final act.

Points of Dissimilarity

Two significant points of dissimilarity are those of the relationship to Messianic expectation and the exercise of divine authority. Jesus as ὁ υἱὸς τοῦ ἀνθρώπου exhibits strong links to messianic expectation and exercises divine authority during both his earthly ministry and, especially so in the eschaton. Ezekiel's authority extends only to him being an agent of divine revelation, to Yahweh's use of him in performing a visionary resurrection and to the laying out of new temple plans as a kind of new Moses. While this is significant, there is no exercise of messianic or divine authority. Both of these themes are almost entirely absent from Ezekiel's role as בֶּן־אָדָם. Messianic expectation is created by Ezekiel's work (esp. ch. 34:23–24), but there is never any suggestion that Ezekiel is the object of that expectation. Ezekiel never has authority as a king/prince and the use of בֶּן־אָדָם deliberately marks him out as merely creature in the presence of his creator. Ezekiel falls face down when he only looks at the human-like one who sits high on the throne above the expanse of the chariot and even this must be considered an act of utter condescension on the part of Yahweh. Indeed, the book of Ezekiel amplifies the presence, power, and initiative of Yahweh to such an extent that all human responsibility (even Ezekiel's himself) is thought by some to be sidelined by the book, at least in its picture of the restoration.[2] To put this point in more modern terms, though his pronouncements and predictions concern both the sacred and secular, Ezekiel himself only has a role in the sacred space as a prophet.[3] Jesus, on the other hand, speaks of a Son of Man who does much more than this. He not only brings the revelation of Yahweh about the Messiah but claims to be the Christ; he not only speaks of theophany but makes himself the subject of it. Therefore, the Markan Son of Man has a strong affinity with messianic expectation and divine authority, while Ezekiel's בֶּן־אָדָם could at best be said to have only a tangential relationship with these concepts.

Conclusion

Burkett's dismissal of an Ezekielic background for ὁ υἱὸς τοῦ ἀνθρώπου raised two final questions that can now be answered: (3) Would a relationship to Ezekiel help to explain Jesus's suffering and death? (4) Would it help to explain the authority of Jesus as a "heavenly witness or judge"? The answer to question three is undoubtedly yes. The significant theme of conflict and rejection at the hands of their fellow Israelites and their leaders is shared by both Jesus and Ezekiel. Both suffer among and on behalf of their people. Both suffer in fulfillment of a divine plan and direction. In response to the latter question, it must be admitted that בֶּן־אָדָם in Ezekiel is not messianic, let alone divine. However, though Ezekiel's role is much more muted than

2. E.g. Joyce, *Divine Initiative*.

3. Even where Ezekiel is asked to "judge" (20:4; 22:2; 23:36) the concept is more one of reproof and the rhetorical effect appears to be the fact that even the lowly בֶּן־אָדָם is able to judge. Cf. Block, *Ezekiel*, 619–20, esp. n. 42; Greenberg, *Ezekiel 1–20*, 363.

anything that Jesus claims for ὁ υἱὸς τοῦ ἀνθρώπου, both sons of man are prophets of destruction of the temple and agents of resurrection. Both Ezekiel and Jesus receive a vindication at the conclusion of their ministry.

Beneath these questions of theme is a significant link based on the core form and use of the phrases. Jesus's use of ὁ υἱὸς τοῦ ἀνθρώπου is the only singular, articular use of a "son of man" phrase (and in his case he uses two articles). Ezekiel's is the earliest singular definite use of the phrase. These are among the only examples of definite singular "son of man" phrases (and others are often understood to depend on one or other of them e.g. Daniel 8:17). Moreover, the book of Ezekiel and the Gospel of Mark present בֶּן־אָדָם and ὁ υἱὸς τοῦ ἀνθρώπου as complex nicknames for their subjects. While the nature of those nicknames, and the themes that they relate to may differ, the fact that both are singular, definite nicknames offers a significant point of similarity.

8

Evaluation of the Relationship between the Two Sons of Man

EXAMINATION OF THE RELATIONSHIP between the sons of man in Ezekiel and Mark will necessarily be open to subjective analysis. Aside from the use of a son of man phrase—which is not without significance—there are no hints of quotations (whether formulaic, direct or paraphrased) nor any particular allusion to the book of Ezekiel in the Gospel of Mark. The absence of something more objective, while limiting the decisiveness of conclusions, should not inhibit the discussion of possible links between the two sons of man. "The importance of understanding the OT background to the NT should not be underestimated. Even though . . . numerous difficulties still confront the scholar who addresses such issues, this does not mean that the topic is not worth pursuing."[1]

The central question to be asked at this point is whether Jesus and those who transmitted his teaching display a dependence on Ezekiel or at least intended to convey some kind of link to Ezekiel in the use of Son of Man. If we are to take the Markan witness as credible, this was certainly the case with Daniel, and most probably the case with Psalm 110 and Isaiah's suffering servant. Unlike these examples, however, there is not the same obvious lexeme-based allusion to Ezekiel within individual Son of Man sayings. Moreover, בֶּן־אָדָם in Ezekiel appears to be used to emphasize his humility rather than convey a supreme authority in either the present or the eschaton. Furthermore, since there is also no suggestion of a link to the Messiah in relation to Ezekiel nor some expectation of a prophet like Ezekiel, it cannot be said that Ezekiel exhausts the background for ὁ υἱὸς τοῦ

---

1. Porter, *Sacred Tradition*, 27.

ἀνθρώπου as Jesus used it. Furthermore, if Daniel's vision, Psalm 110, and the suffering servant of Isaiah are taken together as offering background to Jesus's use of the term, then there is a well-rounded picture of Son of Man which provides many of the themes touched on in Mark's account: divine authority, eschatological judgment, suffering, Messiah and scriptural warrant. Thus, even without the addition of Ezekiel to the milieu of the Markan Son of Man, there is significant background already to be explored.

What none of these options offer, however, is an account of why Jesus started using this phrase for himself. Why did he start using "son of man" as a nickname and in such a way that people in later centuries would call it a title? This is where Ezekiel offers one significant possibility for background. At the form and function core, Ezekiel's use of בֶּן־אָדָם offers the only preexisting singular and definite "son of man" phrase and it is used as a kind of nickname. At this most basic level, Jesus may have picked up the idea of referring to himself as ὁ υἱὸς τοῦ ἀνθρώπου from Ezekiel, in a similar way to that evident in Daniel 8:17 which appears to have been influenced by Ezekiel.

There is also similarity in what the appellative conveys since when the two son of man characters are explored further, Ezekiel's בֶּן־אָדָם offers some strong affinity with the metanarrative themes of ὁ υἱὸς τοῦ ἀνθρώπου in Mark. Most importantly, Ezekiel when commissioned is set in conflict with the Israelites and their leaders, which was identified as a major unifying theme of Jesus's Son of Man sayings when they were considered within their context. Furthermore, Ezekiel is also bound, like Jesus, to fulfill God's plans even at cost of his own pain. There are also associated ideas in receiving a final vindication, prophesying about the temple's destruction, and being involved in performing a resurrection. Thus, both the core idea of using "son of man" as a specific appellative and many of the themes related to it as a kind of nickname could have been drawn by Jesus from Ezekiel.

As discussed above there is no impediment in regard to language or awareness of Ezekiel to preclude it as background. Ezekiel's position within the established Hebrew canon, the reading of his text, and the comprehensibility of his language should not be questioned. Therefore, it would be reasonable to conclude that Jesus knew Ezekiel and could have expected his Jewish listeners to know it as well. The Gospel writers would also in turn be able to expect their readers to become aware of such a work if they were not already. Jesus would have been completely free to draw on Ezekiel and make nuanced links to his Son of Man theme and expect his hearers to notice them.

It is possible that a link to Ezekielic background could help solve a number of the issues of the Son of Man problem, aside from the background itself. For example, it could help explain why Son of Man never becomes a confessional title in the New Testament. That is, as in Ezekiel, it is simply a quirky turn of phrase used by a particular person with a particular meaning. In Jesus's case it appears to be honorific, at least in the end when he ties it specifically to the divine authority witnessed in the Danielic vision, while in Ezekiel's case it is (for want of a better phrase) a dis-honorific, consigning him to the realm of humanity compared with the splendor of Yahweh. Within their respective narratives, however, both בֶּן־אָדָם and ὁ υἱὸς τοῦ ἀνθρώπου never become titles but they are titular in the sense that they come to stand for who and what their respective subject is in their own person and role before God and humanity.

It also gives further credence to the distancing and parable-like view of ὁ υἱὸς τοῦ ἀνθρώπου through the earthly ministry of Jesus. That is, it offers a plausible explanation for why Jesus would and could have used this particular phrase to make seemingly lofty public claims about himself. For he was mixing a lofty Danielic/Aramaic Son of Man, with a lowly human Ezekielic/Hebrew son of man with themes found in Deutero-Isaiah and the messianic Psalms. Neither son of man figure was particularly an object of hopeful expectation at the time, and by innovation Jesus would have been free to build the picture as he saw fit and combine it with messianic and Isaianic themes. Additionally, since it is woven from such disparate threads, Jesus would have had plausible deniability while building the complex picture of his enigmatic self-designation early on should anyone attempt to make accusations or even anoint him as an earthly king by drawing too heavily on one or other of the backgrounds being combined.

This would also then give credence to the view that Jesus's use of the phrase, which could always be understood as a basic circumlocution for himself, was nonetheless quite peculiar from the start, more unusual even than Ezekiel's use since he applied it to himself. Of course, Jesus expected that once he had built up the connotations of the phrase, rival teachers would seek to put him to death—and this is expected according to the Ezekielic thread. By the time the picture had been completed, Jesus's loyal followers would not have thought of anyone else as Son of Man, but nor would they have thought of it as occurring elsewhere than on the lips of Jesus.

Since understanding what Jesus meant by Son of Man is significant for much of New Testament theology, further explorations of what has been raised in this study might lead to some significant findings. It could, for example, offer some insight into the significance of Jesus's role as an agent of God especially as it relates to his divinity.[2] Similarly, it may offer insight

---

2. See for discussion Bauckham, *God Crucified*.

into the significance of Jesus's acceptance of worship.³ It could even cast light on whether there might be a trajectory of God's progressive condescension, or a distinction within God, or a separation of the agency of God developed through the Old Testament and into the New.⁴ Thus, beyond what can even begin to be described in this study, a deeper and fuller understanding of the relationship between the sons of man in Ezekiel and Mark may offer some insight on Christology and the development of Trinitarian understandings of God.

The only conclusion that can be drawn from the entirety of the preceding argument is that Ezekiel could plausibly, at some level, have formed the background for Jesus's Son of Man motif. This does not mean that Jesus was definitely informed by Ezekiel and his use of the phrase, but it does mean that any New Testament scholarship which has too quickly overlooked or put aside Ezekiel in favor of the more popular texts has done this critical topic for understanding Jesus and his own self-awareness a disservice. As BDAG put it, "Much neglected in the discussion is the probability of prophetic association suggested by the form of address Ezk 2:1 al. (like the OT prophet [Ezk 3:4–11] Jesus encounters resistance)."⁵ A number of links have been raised in this book, and there may well be more besides them, but fuller and deeper exploration and evaluation of them could form a significant avenue for further research. Most significantly however, since this book only dealt with Mark's Gospel, attention should be drawn to the other Synoptic sources as well as John's Gospel, since the themes and relationships found here should hold across them. While ultimate certainty about Jesus's dependence on Ezekiel may elude this enquiry it is plausible to concur with Sidebottom, who wrote in 1961 that Jesus may have pieced together a concept of Son of Man from many parts of the Old Testament and that it "is hard to resist the conclusion that Ezekiel was one of the sitters for the composite portrait."⁶ Once these links have been more thoroughly explored and evaluated attention can turn to the questions of the Son of Man problem. As with most research, for as many questions about the historical

---

3. Hurtado speaks of the significance of worship of Jesus as a marker of his divinity, but Collins notes that this may have been an appropriate way of relating to one considered messianic. Hurtado, *How on Earth*, 47–48; Hurtado, *One God*, 12–16; Hurtado, *Lord Jesus*, 29–53; Collins and Collins, *King and Messiah*, 211–12; Collins, "How on Earth," 55–66.

4. Rowland, for example, argues that Dan 7:13–14 is a final stage of a distinction between the human-like figure of Ezek 1:26. Rowland, *Open Heaven*, 96–98; cf. discussion of this in Kanagaraj, *Mysticism*, 163–65, 175–78.

5. BDAG, s.v. "υἱός", γ. ὁ υἱὸς τοῦ ἀνθρώπου.

6. Sidebottom, *Fourth Gospel*, 78.

concerns, the form, the inherent meaning of the phrase and its background which might be answered, there will probably be as many more that can be asked.

9

Final Conclusion

THIS BOOK HAS SOUGHT to examine the meaning of ὁ υἱὸς τοῦ ἀνθρώπου in Mark's Gospel and determine whether, contrary to the general perception in scholarship, the book of the prophet Ezekiel may offer some background for this phrase.

There are three main reasons why Ezekiel may have been overlooked: (1) the background already on offer in Daniel, as well as the Psalms and Isaiah, have provided substantial avenues for research and debate; (2) the lack of consensus regarding the language of Jesus and lack of confidence of his familiarity regarding both Hebrew and Greek, which meant Ezekiel might have been an unlikely candidate for background and which also raised questions as to what ὁ υἱὸς τοῦ ἀνθρώπου was trying to convey; and (3) the common practice of examining the Son of Man sayings outside of their literary context in the Gospel narrative, which meant that the unifying theme of conflict and rejection may have been overlooked. In response, this book has argued: (1) that the background offered by Daniel, the Psalms, and Isaiah does not preclude the possibility of a further background and does little to account for the use of the designation as an honorific; (2) that what is now understood of the cultural-linguistic situation of the first century allows for Jesus to be familiar with both Hebrew (Ezekiel had a well-established place in the Hebrew canon) and Greek; and (3) that the Son of Man sayings should not be divorced from the context in which the Gospels present them, since there is no other context in which they can be examined. Thus, dismissing or overlooking Ezekiel as a possible background on these common grounds should no longer continue.

By working through each example of the phrase ὁ υἱὸς τοῦ ἀνθρώπου in Mark's Gospel it was established that the phrase was used only by Jesus and exclusively about himself as kind of self-chosen honorific—a nickname which captured who he was and what he did. The public nature and identifiable subject of this Son of Man makes it very different to the "son of man" figure found in the Similitudes of Enoch. There are three broad phases of time with which the Son of Man sayings deal: the present, in which the Son of Man exercises divine authority, the imminent future, in which the Son of Man will be rejected, killed, and rise again, and the eschaton, in which the Son of Man is to appear in theophanic glory. There are three further themes that can be found in most of the episodes in which a Son of Man saying occurs. The first is the link with prophecy, where Jesus makes clear connection with Davidic expectation, gives scriptural warrant for his impending fate (probably including Isaiah's suffering servant), and draws on Daniel 7 (and probably Psalm 110) to speak of his final glory. The second theme is that of Messiah whereby Jesus ties together issues of Messiah and Son of God to Son of Man in each of the three categories of sayings. The Gospel's "kingdom of God" theme is also thus united to the Son of Man though direct language of kingdom is used only occasionally in the Son of Man episodes. The third theme is that of conflict and rejection. Every Son of Man saying, when read in its episode, portrays the Son of Man (and at times his elect) in conflict with others. This theme might also deliberately bookend Mark's use of the phrase in his Gospel: Jesus is first thought blasphemous by some scribes just before Jesus's first Son of Man saying, and finally condemned for blasphemy by the Sanhedrin just after the last Son of Man saying.

What Ezekiel potentially offers in terms of background comes at the most basic form-function level and resonates with themes at the broadest level. At the basic level Ezekiel offers an example of the use of a "son of man" phrase as a kind of nickname and it is the only example of a singular and definite use of the term before the ὁ υἱὸς τοῦ ἀνθρώπου of the New Testament. In examining the broadly connected themes, both בֶּן־אָדָם and ὁ υἱὸς τοῦ ἀνθρώπου are set in conflict with the leaders of the Jewish people and fulfill God's plans even to their own detriment. Both also receive some final vindication, prophesy about the temple's destruction, and are involved in resurrections.

Ezekiel cannot account for the divine authority of ὁ υἱὸς τοῦ ἀνθρώπου or its association with the Messiah. The Hebrew/Ezekiel phrase is far more humble than the Aramaic/Daniel one, and has no direct relationship with a concept of Davidic Messiah. Accepting Ezekiel would not at all diminish, however, the background to be found in Daniel 7, nor that in Isaiah nor that probably found in the Psalms. This contrast of background could, however, help explain how and why Jesus was able to use the phrase publicly, and yet without arousing (too much early) suspicion. Jesus may have been deliberately combining the contrasting images of a humble, suffering-rejection "son of man" from Ezekiel, with the glorified, judgment-executing Son of Man from Daniel (with Christ and suffering servant thrown into the package as well).

The impact such a relationship with Ezekiel would have on the Son of Man problem is broad. For example: Does this help to explain how the singular definite form was chosen for the phrase? Does relationship with Ezekiel give plausible reasons for why the phrase did not become a true christological title in the New Testament? Does it help to explain why ὁ υἱὸς τοῦ ἀνθρώπου is only ever used of Jesus and almost exclusively by Jesus in the New Testament? These issues have been touched on in the discussion above but need much more thorough examination. Further, while an argument for the possible background for Daniel's use of "son of man" language was suggested, it was not thoroughly explored. Dependency is evident in 8:17 and perhaps also in chapter 7, but how that more distant background might possibly color Jesus's fulfillment of the Danielic vision is a further point for enquiry. Moreover, there is scope for a biblical-theology examination of this topic, that is, examining a development of "son of man" (and related concepts and themes) through the Old Testament Scriptures and finding its fulfillment in Christ. The biggest avenue for further study would be the comparison to the Son of Man material in Matthew and Luke as well as John.

Sidebottom's conclusion that it "is hard to resist the conclusion that Ezekiel was one of the sitters for the composite portrait" which Jesus painted of himself as Son of Man,[1] may not be agreed to by all. However, this study has shown that the relationship between the sons of man in Ezekiel and Mark may be deeper than most scholars have acknowledged. At the very least, this study has shown the prudence of the translators of the NIV2011, who in justifying their translation of Ezekiel 2:1 wrote this footnote: "The Hebrew phrase ben adam means human being. The phrase son of man is retained as a form of address here and throughout Ezekiel because of its possible association with 'Son of Man' in the New Testament."

---

1. Sidebottom, *Fourth Gospel*, 78.

Bibliography

Allison, Dale C., Jr. *The Historical Christ and the Theological Jesus*. Grand Rapids, MI: Eerdmans, 2009.

Athas, George, and Ian M. Young. *Elementary Biblical Hebrew: An Introductory Grammar*. 4th ed. Croydon Park: Ancient Vessel, 2013.

Bartelmus, Rüdiger. "Mk 2,27 und die ältesten Fassungen des Arbeitsruhegebotes im AT: Biblisch-theologische Beobachtungen zur Sabbatfrage." *BN* 41 (1988) 41–64.

Bauckham, Richard. *God Crucified: Monotheism and Christology in the New Testament*. Grand Rapids, MI: Eerdmans, 1998.

Beckwith, Roger T. *The Old Testament Canon of the New Testament Church and its Background in Early Judaism*. Grand Rapids, MI: Eerdmans, 1986.

Bèze, Théodore de. *Novum Testamentum Domini Nostri Jesu Christi*. New York: D. Appleton & Co., 1848.

Block, Daniel I. *The Book of Ezekiel, Chapters 1–24*. NICOT. Grand Rapids, MI: Eerdmans, 1997.

Bock, Darrell L. "Blasphemy and the Jewish Examination of Jesus." *BBR* 17, no. 1 (2007) 53–114.

Bolt, Peter. *The Cross from a Distance: Atonement in Mark's Gospel*. NSBT. Downers Grove, IL: IVP, 2004.

———. *Jesus' Defeat of Death: Persuading Mark's Early Readers*. SNTSMS. Cambridge: Cambridge University Press, 2003.

Broadhead, Edwin K. *Naming Jesus: Titular Christology in the Gospel of Mark*. JSNTSup. Sheffield: Sheffield Academic, 1999.

Brooks, James A. *Mark*. NAC. Nashville: Broadman & Holman, 1991.

Brownlee, William Hugh. *Ezekiel 1–19*. WBC, vol. 28. Dallas: Word, 1986.

Bullock, C. Hassell. "Ezekiel, Bridge between the Testaments." *JETS* 25, no. 1 (March 1, 1982) 23–31.

Bultmann, Rudolf. *The History of the Synoptic Tradition*. Translated by John Marsh. Oxford: Blackwell, 1963.

Burkett, Delbert Royce. *The Son of Man Debate: A History and Evaluation*. SNTSMS. Cambridge: Cambridge University Press, 1999.

Campbell, Constantine R. *Basics of Verbal Aspect in Biblical Greek*. Grand Rapids, MI: Zondervan, 2008.

———. *Verbal Aspect and Non-Indicative Verbs: Further Soundings in the Greek of the New Testament*. Studies in Biblical Greek, vol. 15. New York: Peter Lang, 2008.

———. *Verbal Aspect, the Indicative Mood, and Narrative: Soundings in the Greek of the New Testament*. Studies in Biblical Greek, vol. 13. New York: Peter Lang, 2007.

Caragounis, Chrys C. *The Son of Man: Vision and Interpretation*. Tübingen: Mohr, 1986.

Casey, Maurice. *Aramaic Sources of Mark's Gospel*. Cambridge: Cambridge University Press, 1999.

———. *The Solution to the "Son of Man" Problem*. London: T. & T. Clark, 2009.

Charlesworth, James H. *Jesus within Judaism*. London: SPCK, 1989.

Collins, Adela Yarbro. "'How on Earth Did Jesus Become a God?' A Reply." In *Israel's God and Rebecca's Children: Christology and Community in Early Judaism and Christianity*, 55–66. Waco, TX: Baylor University Press, 2007.

———. *Mark: A Commentary*. Hermeneia. Minneapolis: Fortress, 2007.

Collins, Adela Yarbro, and John J. Collins. *King and Messiah as Son of God: Divine, Human, and Angelic Messianic Figures in Biblical and Related Literature*. Grand Rapids, MI: Eerdmans, 2008.

Collins, John J. *Daniel: A Commentary on the Book of Daniel*. Hermeneia. Minneapolis: Fortress, 1993.

Crossley, James G. *The Date of Mark's Gospel: Insight from the Law in Earliest Christianity*. JSNTSup. London: T. & T. Clark, 2004.

Culpepper, R. Alan. *Mark*. SHBC. Macon, GA: Smyth & Helwys, 2007.

Davies, W. D., and Dale C. Allison. *A Critical and Exegetical Commentary on the Gospel According to Saint Matthew*, vol. 2. Edinburgh: T. & T. Clark, 1988.

Dodd, C. H. *The Founder of Christianity*. London: Macmillan, 1970.

Driver, Samuel Rolles. "Son of Man." In *A Dictionary of the Bible: Dealing with its Language, Literature, and Contents including the Biblical Theology*. Edited by James Hastings. New York: T. & T. Clark, 1911.

Duguid, Iain M. *Ezekiel*. NIVAC. Grand Rapids, MI: Zondervan, 1999.

———. *Ezekiel and the Leaders of Israel*. Leiden: E. J. Brill, 1994.

Dunn, James D. G. *Jesus, Paul and the Law: Studies in Mark and Galatians*. London: SPCK, 1990.

Edwards, James R. *The Gospel According to Mark*. PNTC. Grand Rapids, MI: Eerdmans, 2002.

Ehrman, Bart D. *How Jesus Became God: The Exaltation of a Jewish Preacher from Galilee*. San Francisco: Harper Collins, 2014.

Eichrodt, Walther. *Ezekiel: A Commentary*. The Old Testament Library. London: SCM, 1970.

Ellens, J. Harold. *The Son of Man in the Gospel of John*. New Testament Monographs. Sheffield: Sheffield Phoenix, 2010.

Evans, Craig A. *Mark 8:27–16:20*. WBC, vol. 34B. Dallas: Word, 2001.

Fanning, Buist M. *Verbal Aspect in New Testament Greek*. Oxford Theological Monographs. Oxford: Clarendon, 1990.

Focant, Camille. *The Gospel According to Mark: A Commentary*. Translated by Leslie Robert Keylock. Eugene, OR: Pickwick, 2012.

Fox, Michael V. "The Rhetoric of Ezekiel's Vision of the Valley of the Bones." *HUCA* 51 (1980) 1–15.

Fox Sports. "Anthony Mundine Is Still Desperately Upset That His Rugby League Rep Career Was Cut Short." *Fox Sports*, December 13, 2016. https://www.foxsports.com.au/boxing/anthony-mundine-is-still-desperately-upset-that-his-rugby-league-rep-career-was-cut-short/news-story/cfc23d9e5c2a1870093fcc96fafad3fe.

France, R. T. *The Gospel of Mark: A Commentary on the Greek Text*. NIGTC. Grand Rapids, MI: Eerdmans, 2002.

Freyne, Seán. *Jesus, a Jewish Galilean: A New Reading of the Jesus Story*. London: T. & T. Clark, 2004.

Fuller, Reginald H. "Die Entchristologisierung des Menschensohnes: Die Übertragung des Traditionsgefüges um den Menschensohn auf Jesus." *JBL* 109, no. 4 (December 1, 1990) 721–23.

Garland, David E. *A Theology of Mark's Gospel: Good News about Jesus the Messiah, the Son of God*. Grand Rapids, MI: Zondervan, 2015.

Gleaves, G. Scott. *Did Jesus Speak Greek?: The Emerging Evidence of Greek Dominance in First-Century Palestine*. Eugene, OR: Pickwick, 2015.

Gowan, Donald E. *Theology of the Prophetic Books: The Death and Resurrection of Israel*. Louisville, KY: Westminster John Knox, 1998.

Greenberg, Moshe. *Ezekiel 1–20*. AB. Garden City, NY: Doubleday, 1983.

———. *Ezekiel 21–37*. AB. New York: Doubleday, 1997.

Grimm, Werner. *Weil Ich Dich Liebe: die Verkündigung Jesu und Deuterojesaja*. Bern: Herbert Lang, 1976.

Grindheim, Sigurd. *Christology in the Synoptic Gospels: God or God's Servant?* New York: T. & T. Clark, 2012.

———. *God's Equal: What Can We Know about Jesus' Self-Understanding?* LNTS. London: Bloomsbury, 2013.

Grundmann, Walter. "Χριστός in Paul's Epistles." In *TDNT*, edited by Gerhard Kittel and Gerhard Friedrich, translated by Geoffrey W. Bromiley, 9.540–62. Grand Rapids, MI: Eerdmans, 1974.

Guelich, Robert A. *Mark 1–8:26*. WBC, vol. 34A. Dallas: Word, 1998.

Gundry, Robert H. *Mark: A Commentary on His Apology for the Cross*. Grand Rapids, MI: Eerdmans, 1993.

Haag, H. "בֶּן־אָדָם." In *TDOT*, edited by G. Johannes Botterweck and Helmer Ringgren, 2.159–65. Grand Rapids, MI: Eerdmans, 1975.

Hartman, Louis Francis, and Alexander A. Di Lella. *The Book of Daniel*. AB, vol. 23. Garden City, NY: Doubleday, 1978.

Hengel, Martin. "'Christos' in Paul." In *Between Jesus and Paul: Studies in the Earliest History of Christianity*, 65–77. Philadelphia: Fortress, 1983.

Higgins, Angus J. B. *Jesus and the Son of Man*. London: Lutterworth, 1964.

Hooker, Morna D. *A Commentary on the Gospel According to St. Mark*. BNTC. London: A. & C. Black, 1991.

———. *The Son of Man in Mark*. London: SPCK, 1967.

Hurtado, Larry W. *How on Earth Did Jesus Become a God?: Historical Questions about Earliest Devotion to Jesus*. Grand Rapids, MI: Eerdmans, 2005.

———. *Lord Jesus Christ: Devotion to Jesus in Earliest Christianity*. Grand Rapids, MI: Eerdmans, 2003.

———. *One God, One Lord: Early Christian Devotion and Ancient Jewish Monotheism*. 3rd ed. Cornerstones. London: T. & T. Clark, 2015.

———. "Summary and Concluding Observations." In *"Who Is This Son of Man?": The Latest Scholarship on a Puzzling Expression of the Historical Jesus*, edited by Larry W. Hurtado and Paul Owen, 159–77. LNTS. London: T. & T. Clark, 2010.

Hurtado, Larry W., and Paul Owen, eds. *"Who Is This Son of Man?": The Latest Scholarship on a Puzzling Expression of the Historical Jesus*. LNTS. London: T. & T. Clark, 2010.

Joyce, Paul M. *Divine Initiative and Human Response in Ezekiel*. Sheffield: Bloomsbury, 1989.

Kanagaraj, Jey J. *Mysticism in the Gospel of John: An Inquiry into Its Background*. JSNTSup. Sheffield: Sheffield Academic, 1998.

Lane, William L. *The Gospel of Mark*. NICNT. Grand Rapids, MI: Eerdmans, 1974.

Leiman, Sid Z. *The Canon and Masorah of the Hebrew Bible: An Introductory Reader*. New York: Ktav, 1974.

———. *The Canonization of Hebrew Scripture: The Talmudic and Midrashic Evidence*. Hamden: Achon, 1976.

Lim, Timothy H. *The Formation of the Jewish Canon*. ABRL. New Haven: Yale University Press, 2013.

Lindars, Barnabas. *Jesus, Son of Man: A Fresh Examination of the Son of Man Sayings in the Gospels in the Light of Recent Research*. Grand Rapids, MI: Eerdmans, 1983.

Lukaszewski, Albert L. "Issues Concerning the Aramaic Behind ὁ υἱὸς τοῦ ἀνθρώπου." In *"Who Is This Son of Man?": The Latest Scholarship on a Puzzling Expression of the Historical Jesus*, edited by Larry W. Hurtado and Paul Owen, 1–27. LNTS. London: T. & T. Clark, 2010.

Lust, Johan. "Ezekiel Manuscripts in Qumran: Preliminary Edition of 4Q Ez a and b." In *Ezekiel and His Book: Textual and Literary Criticism and their Interrelation*, edited by Johan Lust, 90–100. BETL. Leuven: Leuven University Press, 1986.

Manning, Gary T. *Echoes of a Prophet: The Use of Ezekiel in the Gospel of John and in Literature of the Second Temple Period*. JSNTSup. London: T. & T. Clark, 2004.

Marcus, Joel. *Mark 1–8*. AB. New Haven: Yale University Press, 2000.

———. *Mark 8–16*. AB. New Haven: Yale University Press, 2000.

Marshall, I. Howard. *The Origins of New Testament Christology*. Updated ed. Leicester: Apollos, 1990.

———. "Son of Man." In *Dictionary of Jesus and the Gospels*, edited by Joel B. Green, Scot McKnight, 775–81. Downers Grove, IL: IVP, 1992.

McClymond, Michael J. *Familiar Stranger: An Introduction to Jesus of Nazareth*. Grand Rapids, MI: Eerdmans, 2004.

McCown, Chester Charlton. "Luke's Translation of Semitic into Hellenistic Custom." *JBL* 58 no. 3 (1939) 213–20.

Millard, A. R. *Reading and Writing in the Time of Jesus*. BibSem. Sheffield: Sheffield Academic, 2000.

Miller, Stephen R. *Daniel*. Logos Digital. NAC. Broadman, 1994.

Moloney, Francis J. *The Gospel of Mark: A Commentary*. Peabody, MA: Hendrickson, 2002.

Moule, C. F. D. *Essays in New Testament Interpretation*. Cambridge: Cambridge University Press, 1982.

Müller, Mogens. *The Expression Son of Man and the Development of Christology: A History of Interpretation*. Sheffield: Equinox, 2008.

Murphy, Catherine M. *John the Baptist: Prophet of Purity for a New Age*. Interfaces. Collegeville, MN: Liturgical, 2003.
Naylor, Peter. *A Study Commentary on Ezekiel*. Darlington, England: EP Books, 2011.
Novenson, Matthew V. *Christ among the Messiahs: Christ Language in Paul and Messiah Language in Ancient Judaism*. New York: Oxford University Press, 2012.
Odell, Margaret S. *Ezekiel*. SHBC. Macon, GA: Smyth & Helwys, 2005.
Olley, John W. *Ezekiel: A Commentary Based on Iezekiēl in Codex Vaticanus*. Leiden; Boston: Brill, 2009.
Omanson, Roger L., and Bruce Manning Metzger. *A Textual Guide to the Greek New Testament: An Adaptation of Bruce M. Metzger's Textual Commentary for the Needs of Translators*. Stuttgart: Deutsche Bibelgesellschaft, 2006.
Ong, Hughson T. *The Multilingual Jesus and the Sociolinguistic World of the New Testament*. Linguistic Biblical Studies, vol. 12. Leiden: Brill, 2016.
Owen, Paul. "Problems with Casey's 'Solution.'" In *"Who Is This Son of Man?": The Latest Scholarship on a Puzzling Expression of the Historical Jesus*, edited by Larry W. Hurtado and Paul Owen, 28–49. LNTS. London: T. & T. Clark, 2010.
Pace, Sharon. *Daniel*. SHBC. Macon, GA: Smyth & Helwys, 2008.
Peterson, Brian Neil. *John's Use of Ezekiel: Understanding the Unique Perspective of the Fourth Gospel*. Minneapolis: Fortress, 2015.
Porter, Stanley E. *Sacred Tradition in the New Testament: Tracing Old Testament Themes in the Gospels and Epistles*. Grand Rapids, MI: Baker Academic, 2016.
———. *When Paul Met Jesus: How an Idea Got Lost in History*. New York: Cambridge University Press, 2016.
Räisänen, Heikki. *"The Messianic Secret" in Mark*. SNTW. Edinburgh: T. & T. Clark, 1990.
Renz, Thomas. *The Rhetorical Function of the Book of Ezekiel*. Boston: Humanities, 2002.
Rowland, Christopher. *The Open Heaven: A Study of Apocalyptic in Judaism and Early Christianity*. New York: Crossroad, 1982.
Runge, Steven E. *Discourse Grammar of the Greek New Testament: A Practical Introduction for Teaching and Exegesis*. Peabody: Hendrickson, 2010.
Sanders, E. P. *The Historical Figure of Jesus*. New York: Penguin, 1993.
Schmidt, Nathaniel. "The 'Son of Man' in the Book of Daniel." *JBL* 19, no. 1 (1900) 22.
Scholten, Wessel. *Specimen hermeneutico-theologicum: De appellatione τοῦ υἱοῦ τοῦ ἀνθρώπου, qua Jesus se Messiam professus est*. Trajecti ad Rhenum: Paddenburg & Schoonhoven, 1809.
Schürer, Emil. *The History of the Jewish People in the Age of Jesus Christ (175 B.C.–A.D. 135)*, vol. 2. Edited by Géza Vermès, Fergus Millar, and Matthew Black. Edinburgh: T. & T. Clark, 1979.
Schweizer, Eduard. "Der Menschensohn (Zur Eschatologischen Erwartung Jesu)." *ZNW* 50 (1959) 185–209.
Seccombe, David Peter. *The King of God's Kingdom: A Solution to the Puzzle of Jesus*. Carlisle: Paternoster, 2002.
Sidebottom, E. M. *The Christ of the Fourth Gospel in the Light of First-Century Thought*. London: SPCK, 1961.
Stein, Robert H. *Mark*. BECNT. Grand Rapids, MI: Baker Academic, 2008.
Steinmann, Andrew. *Daniel*. Saint Louis, MO: Concordia, 2008.
Strauss, Mark L. *Mark*. ZECNT. Grand Rapids, MI: Zondervan, 2014.

Stuhlmacher, Peter. "Vicariously Giving His Life for Many, Mark 10:45 (Matt. 20:28)." In *Reconciliation, Law and Righteousness*, translated by Everett R. Kalin, 16–29. Philadelphia: Fortress, 1986.

Taylor, Joan E. *The Immerser: John the Baptist within Second Temple Judaism*. Grand Rapids, MI: Eerdmans, 1997.

Van Iersel, Bas. *Mark: A Reader-Response Commentary*. London: T. & T. Clark, 2004.

Vanhoye, Albert. "L'utilisation du livre d'Ézéchiel dans l'Apocalypse." *Biblica* 43, no. 3 (1962) 436–76.

Vawter, Bruce Francis. "Ezekiel and John." *CBQ* 26, no. 4 (October 1964) 450–58.

Vermès, Géza. *Jesus the Jew: A Historian's Reading of the Gospels*. London: Collins, 1973.

———. "Present State of the 'Son of Man' Debate." *JJS* 29, no. 2 (September 1, 1978) 123–34.

———. "The 'Son of Man' Debate.'" *JSNT* 1 (October 1, 1978) 19–32.

Wallace, Daniel B. *Greek Grammar Beyond the Basics: An Exegetical Syntax of the New Testament*. Grand Rapids, MI: Zondervan, 1996.

Watson, David F. *Honor among Christians: The Cultural Key to the Messianic Secret*. Minneapolis: Fortress, 2010.

Webb, Robert L. *John the Baptiser and Prophet: A Socio-Historical History*. JSNTSup. Sheffield: JSOT Press, 1991.

Widder, Wendy. *Daniel*. The Story of God Bible Commentary. Grand Rapids, MI: Zondervan, 2016.

Wink, Walter. *John the Baptist in the Gospel Tradition*. SNTSMS. Cambridge: Cambridge University Press, 1968.

Witherington III, Ben. *The Gospel of Mark: A Socio-Rhetorical Commentary*. Grand Rapids, MI: Eerdmans, 2001.

Wrede, William. *The Messianic Secret*. Translated by J. C. G. Greig. Cambridge: James Clarke, 1971.

Zimmerli, Walther. *Ezekiel 2: A Commentary on the Book of the Prophet Ezekiel*. Edited by Frank Moore Cross and Klaus Baltzer. Translated by Ronald E. Clements. Hermeneia. Philadelphia: Fortress, 1979.

www.ingramcontent.com/pod-product-compliance
Lightning Source LLC
Chambersburg PA
CBHW070931160426
43193CB00011B/1660